THE GREEN MAN
true stories of a paramedic
from the roadside

RON GILLATT, FASI FICAP
Based on his real life progression from Ambulanceman to
a Professional Paramedic in Great Britain (1960s to 1990s)

Gillatt, Ronald   1945 –
The Green Man: True Stories of a Paramedic from the Roadside – 1st ed.

ISBN 978-1-9991336-0-3 (print)
ISBN 978-1-9991336-1-0 (ebook)

Published in Canada by Green Man Publishing House.
Ron Gillatt; www.rongillatt.com

Cover & Book Design by Carolyn McNall.
Front Cover Photo courtesy Ron Gillatt.
Back Cover Photo by Ted McLauchlin.

This book is dedicated to all the Emergency Services personnel everywhere, for your hard work, your professionalism, and your devotion to your calling, particularly those who suffer in silence, maybe for years, because of the mental trauma of emergency work.

Thank you for caring.

Table of Contents

Prologue

The Green Man has been written because after a great many years since leaving the Ambulance Service in Great Britain, I was diagnosed with PTSD (Post-Traumatic Stress Disorder). This was as a result of being exposed to the everyday horrors of working as a paramedic in Great Britain. PTSD has finally started to be recognised as a major problem for first responders such as paramedics, fire fighters and police officers.

The members of these professions probably all have one thing in common and that is, in most cases, we do not talk about our work to our families. We only talk to each other because unless you have been directly involved and worked through the carnage, it would be impossible to know what it's really like. Only your colleagues understand what you are going through. I was always aware that when people would say, "I know how you feel," *they did not*. What would be more correct for them to say would be something like: "I heard what you said but I have no idea what you must be going through."

I chose to put this book content in autobiographical form. It is the fact-based account of the day-to-day life I led between 1967 and 1998, during my thirty-one year career in the UK Ambulance Service. Readers should be advised that there are some very graphic accounts of a number of incidents, some of which may be considered horrific and some that are very sad and may produce a tear.

But I can tell you, it is all true. The stories and experiences described are seen through my own eyes and the details are drawn from my recollections and the diary notes I wrote over the years. As such, *The Green Man* is not intended as an historical book but more as an easy read of an interesting and exciting life at a time when the modern world was undergoing incredible changes.

So while the facts are the facts, I will say that all the names of real people have been changed except mine as the author. All incidents recounted are accurate as far as written records and memory allow. Place names have mostly not been changed. No patient is referred to by name in order to preserve patient confidentiality.

As you dig into this book, you will be exposed to a first-hand look at the day-to-day challenges faced by paramedics and also gain insight into the vast changes that occurred in the ambulance service in Great Britain over the three decades that this book covers. I must say it was exciting to be in on the ground floor when structured ambulance service training was just developing. Before that, we were basically just a transport service for the injured, the ill, the dying and the deceased.

However, once we were offered professional-style training in innovative life-saving machines and techniques, *everything changed.* We became part of the first wave of paramedics that propelled ambulance services in the UK, and indeed around the world, into the incredible professional paramedic service that you find in developed countries today.

Still, despite the many innovations, first responders are still at risk of developing PTSD because we cannot save everyone and we still have to walk into dangerous and horrific situations with our heads, our hearts and our training all on high alert.

That being said, it is my hope that this book will provide insight into the formation of this fascinating career path and that it will also enlighten relatives and friends of emergency service professionals about the work their loved ones do and in particular, the horrors facing paramedics on a daily basis.

Meet the Author

My name is Ron Gillatt. I was born in Manchester, England in 1945. After leaving secondary school with a basic education when I was 15, I started a five-year apprenticeship as a motor mechanic at one of the largest Ford dealers in England.

In 1962, when I was 17, I joined the Auxiliary Fire Service (AFS) which was part of the Manchester City Fire Brigade and I became a volunteer fireman. The training was tough and it was strict, very regimental. But it was to be the foundation for the rest of my life.

After completing basic training, I was sent along with other volunteers to different fire stations for our duties. We attended incidents alongside the full-time firemen and did some training and drills with them as well. Although at the time I did not know it, the AFS was to shape my life for many, many years to come.

I gained a lot of practical hands-on experience while attending those emergencies and started to realise that emergency work was in fact what I would like to do full-time. I resigned from the AFS in 1967 and left the Ford dealership in order to pursue a new career in ambulance services.

When I joined the City of Manchester Ambulance Service in 1967, I was a *newcomer*. The first few weeks of working in that environment were such a shock to the system that many recruits did not stick with it. The calls we attended could be brutal and sometimes violent, and many times, it was sad beyond belief. Personally I found the round-the-clock shift work to be quite an adjustment, because it was nothing like working in the garage. But despite it all, I knew this was the right career for me.

My years in the ambulance service were influenced by many events and I enjoyed choosing specific stories and experiences to highlight in this book. Over a period of years, I studied for various professional qualifications in evening classes taken at college and this eventually led to a promotion in 1976. Those qualifications included extensive knowledge of anatomy, physiology, rescue, and advanced patient care.

Then in the early 1980s, local training was made available in nearby hospitals which introduced us to defibrillation, intubation and intravenous infusion. At the time, this was called *extended training* and it was the forerunner of what would eventually be taught as part of paramedic training courses in the UK. In 1989, I became one of the first qualified paramedics working for what became the Greater Manchester Ambulance Service.

In 1991, during the first Gulf War, I was asked to join a British Medical Team going to the Iran–Iraq border in order to treat thousands of people who were displaced by the war. That was an incredible and life-changing experience, and those stories are the makings of perhaps another book.

After returning from the Gulf, I resumed my normal duties. Then in 1993, following a serious back injury, I took up a post of 'tutor' in the Training School where I developed and delivered emergency training to the industry. It was a very fulfilling way to complete my career with the ambulance service. In 1998, I left the service after thirty-one fantastic years.

Since I could not imagine actually retiring in any way, I started my own training company in England in 1998 and transferred that business to Ontario, Canada in 2001. I thoroughly enjoyed 20 years running that very busy international training company until my retirement in early 2018.

Our lives in Woodstock, Ontario continue to be busy but in new and different ways. I have time to pursue my woodworking and I enjoy trap shooting. Without shift-work and so much travel, I now have more time for family gatherings and I also have time to dust off my diaries and peck away, putting stories on paper and sharing them online. I hope you enjoy reading about these stories and developments. It was a career that was lived with excitement and fulfilment, each and every day.

1. The Green Man

On the way to my very first emergency call, my colleague Paul had told me that this was an *unusual* call. Not an emergency call but a 'special'. I had no idea what a 'special' was but I was soon to find out. My shift was 1300 until 2200 hours, which was known as *lates*. This was my first call on my first ever shift and I was eager to get involved.

I had joined the Ambulance Service on April 24, 1967 and my first active day was May 7. I had earned a First Aid Certificate with the fire brigade which was also the required qualification for an ambulanceman in those days. I was assigned to be part of a two-man crew attending various calls, emergencies and non-emergency calls.

We had been requested by the police to attend at an address on Cooper Street in Bradford, a district of Manchester. No bells or flashing lights were needed.

We pulled up outside a rundown *two up-two down* house on a street which was slowly being demolished in order to make way for more modern housing to be built. The term *two up-two down* was used to describe the old houses, most of which were over a hundred years old and were common in this and many parts of Great Britain in the 60s. There were two bedrooms upstairs and two rooms downstairs and most had outside toilets.

A police officer who walked that beat had called us because the only occupant of the house had not been seen for several weeks. The police officer told Paul that he had broken in and saw a body in the back bedroom, so we were called to move that body to the mortuary. Paul told me to wait outside while he went into the house to look at the situation. I was amazed at how many flies were coming out of the open front door. There were thousands.

Paul came out of the house looking very grim and told me that it was a body and since it was in a severe state of decay, I should go and look for myself, in case I was going to vomit! The smell coming from the house and the masses of flies was almost unbearable even on the street and it became more so as I went upstairs to look for myself. I went into the back bedroom and it took me a few moments to realize what I was looking at.

There, lying on a bed, was the dead body and he had clearly decayed substantially to the point that he had turned a very pale green during that process. The smell was overpowering and I was shocked at what I was seeing, even more so when I saw all the maggots that were crawling on the man and on the bed. This was the first time I had been so close to an actual body, let alone one in this state of decay.

I did not vomit but quickly retreated downstairs and out of the house, away from that unbelievable smell and the flies.

"How are you feeling?" Paul asked.

"Bloody hell, I'm glad I'm out of there. The stink and the maggots are making my skin crawl! What are we actually here for? He is clearly dead," I said to Paul.

"We are moving the body to the mortuary," Paul responded in a matter of fact way. "Let's move everything that we don't need in the back of the ambulance and put that stuff in the cab, away from the maggots and any fluid that will probably leak out of him."

"Are you serious?" I asked in disbelief.

"Yes, that's why we are here. We get him certified first and then on to the mortuary."

Then it occurred to me: *This was the 'special' Paul had spoken about on the way over there!*

In those days, it was the ambulance service's job to move most dead bodies. The thought of moving the body made me cringe and shudder. There were no gloves, masks, aprons or protective equipment of any kind in those days so it was bare hands and you had to try to breathe through your mouth.

We tried to wrap the body and maggots in the sheet that he was lying on but it was partially rotted through. After some manoeuvring with old blankets, we eventually had him tightly contained like a "mummy" in a couple of blankets.

"At least that should keep him in one piece and the maggots contained," said Paul. We carried him down the steep stairs and out into the ambulance. I jumped out and Paul closed the back doors.

We took a few minutes in which to get our breath back and do some paperwork with the police officer.

When we both got into the front of the ambulance, we had to open the windows because the smell was so bad you could almost chew it!

Paul picked up the radio since I had not really been taught what to say over the radio yet.

"Alpha 1, over."

"Base, Alpha 1, over."

"Alpha 1 leaving Cooper Street, Bradford for Ancoats Hospital for certification, over."

"Roger Alpha 1, base out."

We were only at the hospital for a couple of minutes and then it was time for the mortuary which was nearby. Paul drove there without saying too much.

"How are you feeling?" Paul asked.

"I'll be OK. Just a bit shocked at this job."

Paul muttered something about it being what we do as we arrived at the mortuary. He went into the building in order to see where the mortuary staff wanted the body.

"OK, let's get him in," said Paul as we placed the stretcher onto a stretcher trolley.

We wheeled the body into the mortuary and helped the attendant slide the body onto the stainless steel table. Paul had warned the staff at the mortuary what to expect and once our delivery was done, we started to get cleaned up. After washing everything down in the back of the ambulance with strong disinfectant, the putrid smell had almost gone. Finally, we had a good wash ourselves and were ready for work again.

"You call the Control Room," said Paul.

"What do I say?" I asked.

"Our call sign is Alpha 1, so tell Control that we are clear at the mortuary."

"Alpha 1 to base, over."

"Base, Alpha 1, over."

"Alpha 1, clear at the mortuary, over."

"Roger Alpha 1. Return to station."

"Alpha 1, roger."

"Base out."

That was my introduction to handling deceased patients. Unfortunately I have handled hundreds of *bodies* since that day: adults, children and babies. Over the following years, as the training started to improve, I became more skilled in how to *save lives* rather than count the number of bodies, but that day, I was just one more new recruit. That first harrowing call was something I never knew existed.

My head was reeling and at the time and I did not know which direction this career would take me. But strangely, I felt that it was a good fit for me. Something new and different every day, *every call.*

At the time, we couldn't do much for the people we attended. There was no training available other than basic first aid qualifications. We did not know it but the British Ambulance Service was about to undergo a transformation that one could hardly imagine. I was along for that ride, it was bumpy in spots, and this is the story as I remember it.

2. Repairing People – Not Cars

When I left school in December 1960, I accepted a five-year apprenticeship as a motor mechanic working for a very busy Ford dealership. During my apprenticeship, I had become more and more disillusioned. I really didn't like always being so dirty and having skinned knuckles and cuts and oil ingrained in my hands, as well as all the other occupational hazards. I did enjoy the car repair business but not the dirt! After I finished my apprenticeship in 1965, I worked as a qualified motor mechanic for a couple of years before looking for a change of career.

Back in 1962, I had joined the Auxiliary Fire Service in Manchester, when I was just seventeen and a half. I really enjoyed my training and my role as a volunteer fireman. I went out on hundreds of different emergency calls working alongside the full-time firemen and meeting members of the police and ambulance services. Because everything in the fire service was done so precisely and according to a predetermined procedure, I had become used to that level of discipline and I realized that was something I thrived on.

One day while at work fixing cars, I was thinking about a serious road accident that I had attended as a volunteer the previous night. The accident was really bad and a number of people were trapped in the wreckage of two cars. It was the fire services' job to cut the casualties out of the wrecked vehicle. The driver of one car looked badly injured with severe lacerations to his face and chest.

At that time, seat belts were only just in their infancy and very few cars were fitted with them. Occupants of cars were just thrown about inside the vehicle during a crash, hence the severe injuries.

I suddenly had a *eureka moment*! That's it, I thought, I will try to join the ambulance service. Those chaps had decent uniforms and there was excitement in their job! This revelation came as a flash, like a bolt of lightning, and I knew in an instant that was what I really wanted to do with my life.

There was an ambulance station nearby where I worked and one lunchtime I wandered into the station to see if I could have a chat with somebody. I got some good advice and found out how to apply to become an ambulanceman. In those days, the ambulance service was definitely not a career, it was just a job. But to me, it was relatively clean, with a nice uniform and according to the ambulancemen that I had spoken to, there was plenty of time off. The more I thought about it, the more it appealed to me. I was looking for some excitement and being able to make decisions, but above all, I wanted a cleaner job and I wanted to work outside.

I wrote to the City of Manchester Ambulance Service in January 1967 to enquire about the recruitment process. I received a fairly quick reply and with it came an application form. The letter said to complete the application and send it in. When vacancies arose, suitable applicants would be notified. I waited weeks after sending it in but heard nothing. I began to wonder if it would work out. In the meantime, I was still working as a mechanic and part-time fireman.

Then I arrived home from work one evening covered in the usual layer of grease and dirt and as I was getting washed, my mother shouted up to me that there was a letter for me and it looked 'official'. I raced downstairs and tore open the envelope not knowing what to expect.

The letter, or to be more precise the 'form', instructed me to attend for an interview at 1400 hours on the 20th March 1967 at the Ambulance Head-quarters, Belle Vue Street, Gorton, Manchester. I was elated! I was just twenty-two and I had the opportunity of fulfilling my desire to become an ambulanceman.

The day of my appointment finally arrived and as I put on my suit, I could not help feeling nervous about the upcoming interview. I just hoped that I would sound sufficiently wise and confident enough to impress my interviewer. Suddenly, a couple of terrible thoughts exploded in my head: "What if there was more than one person doing the interview? How would I cope if they asked me 'trick' questions?"

I regained my composure and I almost marched into the H.Q., chest out, feeling very important and all set to tell everybody, "I am here for an interview for a job to be an Ambulanceman!" But I resisted the temptation and instead, I stared in envy at the men in uniform who were *already* Ambulancemen.

I was shown into a waiting room where I sat down with two other men who were also there for an interview. It had never occurred to me that there could be other people being interviewed for *my* job.

I had been sitting in the waiting room for about two minutes when a door opened and a well-built man of about sixty years of age stood there gazing around the room. He was dressed in uniform and he had two bars on each shoulder, the same rank markings as a Sub Officer in the Fire Service. He also had a bunch of papers in his hand and he kept scanning the papers and then the faces of us three hopefuls who were nervously waiting to be interviewed.

"Good afternoon gentlemen. My name is Albert Brown," he said and his head went down again looking at the papers in his hand and he shook his head. I was becoming more and more nervous when suddenly he said, "Which one of you is Gillatt?"

Oh God, I thought, what has gone wrong? Are they going to dismiss me right now and give *my* job to somebody else?

"Gillatt. Which of you is Ronald Gillatt?" he repeated himself, a bit annoyed.

"That's me, sir," I said with an uneasy tremble in my voice that the others must have heard.

"Come on. Wake up. It's time for your chat with the boss."

Oh hell, I thought, pull yourself together.

"Sorry, I was miles away," I offered as a feeble apology and he grunted acceptance of it. In a split second, I was on my way into an office with lots of photographs of ambulances on the walls. The walls were painted with cream coloured gloss paint and there was a desk at the end of the room. There was also a strong smell of lavender polish in the room. I was ushered to a point about two yards in front of the desk and told to stand there.

Behind the desk sat a thin, middle-aged man. He had gingery grey hair and glasses and he wore a tweed suit rather than a uniform. He looked at the papers that Mr. Brown had given to him and then looked me up and down. I was starting to feel uncomfortable when he announced, "My name is Mr. Huntley and I am the Chief Ambulance Officer." That would be CAO for short.

Bloody hell, I thought, the Chief Officer does not have a uniform. I was expecting the CAO to be like the Chief Fire Officer (CFO) whom I had met during my service with the Auxiliary Fire Service. The CFO was always dressed in a smart black uniform.

I realised I should be concentrating on what the boss was saying. "You are a bit small for this job," he said with a trace of a smirk on his face. I felt unnerved by his remark. At five-foot-four and 116 pounds, I was what I preferred to be described as 'athletic'. Clearly, he had another point of view.

"Sit down," he said. "Tell me about your current job and your AFS work."

I spent several minutes describing my job as a motor mechanic and my spare time role as a volunteer fireman. "Do they just send you to *little fires*?" he asked. I thought it was another sarcastic comment about my size so I did not answer him. He blustered on regardless.

"So, why do you wish to become an Ambulanceman, Mr. Gillatt?"

"Well, Sir, I wish to have a cleaner job, that has good prospects and one where I can make my own decisions and help people." The boss must have heard that corny line – *about helping people* – a thousand times.

"What do you mean, helping people?" he asked.

"Well, I want to er…" I was really unsure of what to say. I knew what I wanted to say but I was unable to describe it.

"Why don't you say that you want to *learn* to be an Ambulanceman?" he offered.

"Yes, that's exactly it, but I did not know how to say it," I fumbled.

By now I was sure that I had probably *not* got the job and although I was disappointed at making such a mess of the interview within the first minute or so, it turned out that our meeting continued on. But by that time, I was no longer trying to impress him, just answering naturally. What was the point? Finally, it came to a close and I felt disappointed it had not gone better. I was relieved it was over.

"Well, thank you for coming along today. We will let you know in a few days," he said, standing up giving me the cue that it was time to go.

"Thank you for seeing me, Sir," I said.

I closed the door behind me and quickly walked out of the Ambulance Station still pondering why I had not known the answers to the questions. As I thought about the interview, I began to analyse what I had said. I *really* did want to help people and I *wanted* to become an Ambulanceman. Surely my interview was not so bad. Surely Mr. Huntley had to see how much I really wanted to work in the Ambulance Service. Still, I worried that I was destined to stay covered in oil, repairing cars and trucks for the rest of my life.

A few days later on the 29th of March, a letter arrived from the City of Manchester Ambulance Service and it simply said: "I am writing to confirm your appointment as a Trainee Ambulanceman with this service. Please report to Ambulance H.Q., Belle Vue at 0800 hrs on Monday 24th April 1967."

I could not believe my eyes. I was an Ambulanceman! Well, I would be in a few weeks' time. I thought that's not very long to swat up on First Aid, splints, and plasters. What else do the ambulances have in them? I racked my brain to try and remember everything that I had seen in the backs of ambulances before. I could not recall seeing anything in the back other than the odd blanket. Why couldn't I seem to picture all that?

Suddenly a voice in my head shouted *stop*. Did the officer at my interview not say, "*Learn* to be an Ambulanceman?" Yes, that's it. They will show me how things are done. I was going to be OK. I just hoped that I could cope with the job and deal with the shift work. Although I had been to many fires which had burned well into the early hours of the morning, I had never actually gone to work at night. I wondered if they had special people to work at night.

All these thoughts whizzed through my head. I was so excited and for the next few weeks I hardly slept. I remember the night before I started work for the Ambulance Service, I didn't sleep at all. I remember that as though it was yesterday.

3. The Pocket-Sized Ambulanceman

Finally the day that I was starting work with the Ambulance Service had arrived and I was there, at Belle Vue Ambulance Station which was the H.Q. of the City of Manchester Ambulance Service. I asked somebody in uniform where he thought I should report to.

"What is it that you want?" he asked with a puzzled look on his face. "Well, I am starting work as an ambulanceman today, and I start at 8 o'clock." The chap then burst into peals of laughter and shouted to other men who were nearby to come over and see the 'Pygmy Ambulanceman'!

I felt very embarrassed and I could feel my face burning red. "Sorry mate, no offence. But you *are* small, aren't you?" he said half apologetically.

"I am five-foot-four and strong as an ox," I said in a voice as confident as I could make it.

"You will have to get used to having the piss taken out of you around here, it happens to us all," he said as he held out his hand. "My name is Ron Green."

"Oh, how strange, my name is Ronald but I prefer Ron," I replied. "Ron Gillatt."

We shook hands and Ron took me over to the office door, showing me the way. I thanked him and as he was leaving, he turned to me and said, "Listen mate, let me give you a bit of advice. There's a saying in the Ambulance Service and that is, if you're still here at the end of your first emergency shift, you'll be here for life. Just try and remember that. It may help you!"

What a strange thing to say, I thought, but I tucked it away.

I knocked on the office door, which was opened by a well-built man in his late fifties or early sixties. He was holding a clipboard and wearing a uniform which had rank markings on the shoulders.

"What is your name?" he asked.

"Ronald Gillatt, Sir."

"You don't call me Sir. I am what is called a Shift Leader not an Officer," he continued. "My name is Albert Brown. You obviously do not remember but we met at your interview."

"Sorry I had not really taken much notice on that occasion," I explained. We shook hands.

"Do you prefer to be called Ronald or Ron?" I told him that I preferred Ron, and he said, "Ron it is then. Well, Ron, welcome to the Ambulance Service."

"Thanks. What do I call you? What's your title?"

"Albert will do just fine," he assured me, as he took me down to the Mess Room for a coffee.

The Mess Room was full to bursting point with dozens of ambulancemen who were about to start their shift. A thick haze of cigarette smoke blanketed the room. There was also the smell of bacon cooking in the kitchen nearby. The room was like a canteen with shiny-topped tables. All the tables had groups of ambulancemen sitting round them and each table had a large teapot or jug of tea on it.

I felt very self-conscious as we entered the room and noticed a few ambulancemen looking at me. I stuck out like a sore thumb because I was the only one not in uniform. I was suddenly aware of a voice somewhere in the room shouting my name.

I eventually traced the voice and was delighted to find that it belonged to Ron Green, the ambulanceman I had met earlier. He again apologised for calling me a 'Pygmy'.

I was not offended, but more embarrassed. He introduced me to a few of the men sitting around his table and they all wished me well. Albert suddenly appeared with two cups of coffee. "Here you are Ron, have a cup of coffee. I take it that you do drink coffee?"

"Now and then I do, thank you," I said.

"When all these noisy sods have gone out, we will fill in the paperwork. You're in the Ambulance Service now and we must make it official by filling in the forms."

By 0815 the room was empty. Everybody had gone out to start their work.

In those days, the majority of the work was taking people to hospital for out-patient appointments. Crews on certain shifts attended the emergency calls.

Once the paperwork was completed, I was taken to the 'stores' in order to be kitted out with everything that a modern Ambulanceman needed! The storeman was named Les and he clearly loved his job. Everything was in various boxes or on open shelves. He could instantly put his hands on anything that was requested from a mop and bucket to forms and uniforms!

Albert introduced me. "Hello Les, this is Ron Gillatt."

"Pleased to meet you, Ron. You are a little chap!"

I felt silly because I was short and they all felt compelled to point it out. Maybe I had picked the wrong job? I was a good motor mechanic, used to doing very heavy work and I never really had any trouble with the fire service. I could run as fast as anybody when needed and I could lift incredible weight for my size. "I am as strong as anybody here," I protested. Les just smiled.

"Shirt size?" 15, I told him.

"Chest size?" 38.

"Inside leg?"

"I don't know."

With a look of delight on his face, Les announced that he would measure my inside leg. Les seem to enjoy doing his measuring a lot more than I did. I learned something about certain men that day! He let out a loud laugh and with a sense of disbelief, he said, "27 inches! We don't have any children's uniforms here!"

Les spent some considerable time finding the uniform items. Some of them, I had to take to be altered in order for them to fit.

After much joking, I was issued with the following items:

- 1 Uniform jacket – black.
- 1 Raincoat – black.

- 1 Pair of trousers – black.

- 1 Uniform cap – shiny peak.

- 1 Cap badge – metal.

- 3 Uniform shirts – blue with detachable collars.

- 1 Pair leather gloves – black.

- 1 Wash leather.

- 1 Tin Simonize wax polish.

- 1 Street guide.

All that was over fifty years ago. Since that day in 1967, I have attended thousands of emergency calls covering the widest variety of incidents you can think of, and maybe some that you could not! They ranged from murders, shootings, air crashes, road accidents, train crashes, suicides, fires, delivering babies, cardiac arrests and many others. The list is endless.

During my interview all those years ago, Mr. Huntley was right when he said that I would *learn* to be an ambulanceman. I was learning every day, because you cannot learn *experience*. Every day was an experience and each incident gave me more experience. In this career, every incident is different because each broken leg is *different*. Nothing is ever the same and it is that variety of work which gives you experience.

After completing my first week as an ambulanceman, I was very con-fused as to who actually dealt with the emergency calls. There must have been some during the week, I thought, but I had not actually seen an ambulance turn out to an emergency call. Also during that first week, there just was no time to think about anything other than all the new stuff such as the uniform, all the various forms to complete, Smallpox and Tetanus injections and many other things like that. We also did a tour of all the hospitals, including all the cafeterias, that I was likely to go to in the Manchester area.

Week Two was taken up with an explanation of how the different shifts worked and the various start times of each shift. I was taken to the 'transport office' at the different hospitals in order to meet the officers who arranged the ambulances to take people home after their hospital appointments. I also made a visit to Manchester Airport and although the airport was actually mostly located in Cheshire County's area, in the event of an emergency with an aircraft, it would be up to the Manchester Ambulance Service to provide additional support.

Finally, on Thursday of my second week of training, I was shown where the 'floating list' was posted every Thursday. The floating list had every ambulanceman's name on it who was not part of a regular crew. There were 22 names on the list and as people eventually got to the top of the list, they were then crewed up with a permanent mate.

This list was where we found out which station we were working at the following week and what shift we were on. There were five stations covering the entire Manchester area. As I checked for my name, I found that I was at the bottom of the list because I was the newest recruit. I could see I was listed as working from 1300 to 2200 at Belle Vue and so the next thing was to find out who I would be working with.

All the ambulances were washed on the outside and mopped out inside at the end of each shift. Then, every six weeks it was polishing day. This was usually on a Sunday day-shift. The ambulance was wax polished from front to back, inside and out. It was very hard work and usually it took all day. When it was polished, it gleamed as though it had just come out of a showroom!

In those days, each Ambulance Service had its own 'livery'. In Manchester all ambulances were a rich maroon colour with shiny black mudguards and front bumpers. Lancashire County ambulances were cream coloured and Cheshire's were a yellowish-cream with beautiful deep blue mudguards and front bumpers. Cheshire ambulances also had their station name either on the cab doors or on the sides of the bodywork.

In Manchester, the regular crews had their own ambulance, which was allocated to them permanently. This led to a great deal of pride and rivalry between crews as to who had the cleanest vehicle. Also every six weeks while working a day-shift, each vehicle got a 'lubrication service' — by its crew! After lunch on the appointed day, overalls were issued by Les in the stores, and the ambulance was driven over the inspection pit.

It was greased all round, the engine oil was changed and all fluid levels checked. After that, the tyres were checked and finally it was given a wash, leathered off with a wash-leather and mopped out in the back and inside the cab. We did all that work ourselves.

Things were very different in those days. Our ambulances were archaic in comparison to the almost luxury of today's vehicles. When I started out, very small revolving blue beacons (lights) had only recently been fitted on the roofs of the ambulances and of course, there were no two-tone horns, sirens or other ear splitting warning devices.

Indeed, all we had was a large, chrome electric bell which was bolted to the front bumper. The driver operated the bell by pressing a switch and as you can imagine, it was almost useless. It sounded like rattling a tin can with a stone in it! Our radios were valve operated and were very limited in efficiency.

The emergency equipment was again almost non-existent when compared with today's 'hospitals on wheels'. The stretchers we used back then were made of wood with a canvas base. On the top of that was a mattress filled with "horse hair" and covered in a washable leather-cloth material. We had two or three blankets that were referred to as 'ex-army blankets' because they were hairy like the old-fashioned military issue ones.

As for equipment, we had an oxygen cylinder which had a rubber pipe, and a rubber mask connected to it. In addition, we had a small first aid box which was not even as well equipped as today's motorist first aid kits.

If you were on 'stand-by duty" which meant that you were just responding to 999 (emergency) calls, then you also had an extra box but it was the same size as the first aid box and this one was placed in the back of the ambulance. The second box was painted bright red and contained a clean sheet to be used as a burn sheet and a contraption called a 'Cardiff Bellows' resuscitator. God knows how it worked! Some of the newer ambulances at that time had carry chairs which was a kind of folding wheelchair type thing which was used to carry patients up and down stairs and to wheel them to the ambulance, however most did not.

Training was in its absolute infancy having only just started to creep into some services as a result of a shake-up by the government. American

MASH units, particularly in Vietnam, were starting to be noticed as to how effective high-quality care could be in the immediate aftermath of injury. So the British government started looking towards better training for ambulance crews in order to deliver more advanced care to patients. The government decided that emergency treatment that was delivered by ambulance services should be nationally organized and standardized.

But when I started out, training consisted of gaining an 'Adult First Aid Certificate' issued by one of the voluntary first aid societies. This qualification had to be earned within one year of commencing work as an ambulanceman. What this really meant was that until you gained a First Aid Certificate, you still worked as an ambulanceman but without any qualification at all!

Most services operated in this same way so the word 'training' was a joke --- because mostly there was none! First Aid classes were organised only occasionally and held at the station one evening each week for a number of weeks. My first instructor was a member of the St. John Ambulance service. His full-time job was as a Postman. He came along each week to teach the assembled ambulance staff how to do their job and covered only the basics of First Aid.

It all seems such a farce now when I look back on it, but that was the standard of training then. After some weeks of attending the sessions, a local doctor would come along to test our knowledge of bandaging and our ability to apply wooden splints. It was always the same doctor, asking the identical questions each time he came to assess a course.

Once you could do those few things, and answer some basic questions about diabetes and epilepsy, a First Aid Certificate was issued which was valid for three years. For this qualification, we received an extra 5 shillings per week which would be 25 pence in today's coinage. I was already in possession of a First Aid Certificate when I joined the ambulance service and the wages I was paid for my first full week was £16: 1s: 8d (sixteen pounds, one shilling, eight pence). My first thoughts when I received my pay packet was, "All this money and I am clean!" It was exciting.

At the end of my second week on the ambulance service, I checked the floating list and found that I would be working with my friend Paul

Dixon. My duty for a full week starting on Sunday was from 1300 hrs until 2200 hrs. As I mentioned before, this was called 'lates'. I was to be part of a crew doing all kinds of ambulance work including 999 calls.

I had known Paul for a few years. We had first met when Paul joined the Auxiliary Fire Service at Moss Side Fire Station, Manchester. I had joined in October 1962. I loved being a volunteer fireman and although we did not receive wages per se, we did get a small payment for each time we attended for duty. Both Paul and I enjoyed turning out to fires and other emergencies alongside the full-time firemen. I know I gained a huge amount of experience attending fires some of which were very big but mostly relatively small, and we got called out to road accidents (some of which were fatal) and various other emergencies.

My involvement with the AFS was 'character forming'. Everything that was done on the drill ground or at an emergency was done as a co-ordinated, well-rehearsed team effort. Everybody had a job to do and we learned to do it *correctly*.

Paul became the Leading Fireman in charge of the crew that I volunteered with. When he eventually joined the Ambulance Service, he left the AFS and that was before I did. We remained good friends and as a result of listening to his stories of incidents that he had attended as an ambulance-man, I was influenced to try and join the Ambulance Service as well.

Paul had been an ambulanceman for about a year and in my inexperienced eyes, he was already an 'expert'! We got on well together and during that week, Paul gave me a good deal of advice that would stay with me for many years. But my greatest test was still to come during that week although I did not know it. Looking back, that week was one of the most traumatic ones in my whole life.

Just sixteen days after walking into Belle Vue Ambulance Station as a very raw, young recruit, I was suddenly on my way to my first *real* 999 call. It was not a 'special' this time but a proper emergency! I had been sitting in the Mess Room having a cup of tea when I heard the bells ringing.

The ringing of the bells was very confusing when you were new. One ring meant that a 'single manned vehicle' was required for walking patients. Two rings were for a crew for a non-emergency job and three rings was for a 999 or emergency call. If you were a newcomer to the service, it was almost impossible to tell what the rings were for. Was that one ring or was it one ring and then two rings or was it really three rings? It just kept on ringing. How the hell could you tell? Plus the bell was used for everything and it was just something you had to learn. So I set about to learn not only how to judge the length of the ring but also keep track if it was our turn to go out. It was all very confusing if you are new to that system. Belle Vue had a great many crews, about 35 in all. They were all doing a mixture of work and of course, not everybody was on station or in the Mess Room so it was impossible to know if there were crews who would be going out before you.

Suddenly, with a loud crash, the Mess Room door was flung open and Paul was standing there holding a piece of paper in his hand. The paper was known as a 'pink' that much I did know. That is because all emergency calls were written down in longhand onto a pink form. My heart began to pound in an uncontrollable way. The Mess Room was quite full and all eyes turned towards the door.

"Didn't you hear the bloody bells?" Paul yelled at me. He was glaring accusingly at me and although I tried to answer him, I found that I just could not speak. I was absolutely petrified at the prospect of attending what I was anticipating was going to be my first 999 call.

"Come on, get a move on," he bellowed. "We've got a kid knocked down by a bus on Great Western Street, Moss Side. Move your bloody self!"

To a growing crescendo of jeers from the men in the Mess Room, I ran after Paul who had already got into the ambulance. I just had time to climb into the passenger's side as we roared off into the traffic. Paul was uttering oaths under his breath and I was trying to tell him that I did not know the system of 'turn out' rings yet. Paul was concentrating on driving and told me to shut up.

The bell on the bumper was clanging away but nobody in traffic could really hear it very well or so it seemed to me. It made driving at that speed very dangerous. I was in such a state I just kept asking Paul what I should do when we arrived at the accident. I had been used to attending emergency calls in the AFS as part of a crew of six where everybody knew what their job was, but now it was just Paul and me and we were the crew. He just kept telling me to shut up while he concentrated on driving.

I don't remember much about the journey to that first Road Traffic Accident which was known as an 'RTA' but I will never forget the scene as we arrived.

There was a huge crowd gathered in the road and Paul got as near as he could. We both jumped out but I really had no idea what I was supposed to be doing. I was running round like a headless chicken not really doing anything at all! This was not like the AFS where everybody knew what everybody else was supposed to do. I could hear Paul bellowing at the crowd telling them to move out of the way. Paul had disappeared into the crowd and being small, I had difficulty forcing my way through to where I thought he was. Finally, I joined Paul and was not prepared for the sight that was waiting for me.

Lying on the road about two feet away from me was a male child aged about ten years old. He was absolutely *pulverised*. The bus had apparently driven over him with its wheels, killing him instantly. This poor mashed, lifeless little body had been someone's child just a few minutes before. Now all I could see was a battered, broken mess of crushed tissue, blood and deformed limbs.

The child was dead. There was no doubt about that but in those days, we had to have dead bodies certified by a doctor at a hospital. Paul was examining the child, but even I knew it was of no use. I was mesmerised by the amount of damage sustained. The wheels had gone over his legs, trunk and head. There were imprints of the tread from the tyres on some of his exposed skin. It was a horrific sight. Suddenly I was aware of Paul asking me to get a blanket from the ambulance and open the rear doors.

I fought my way through the crowd which by then was huge and I opened the rear doors of the ambulance. As I grabbed a blanket, I was aware of being watched by some people in the crowd, some of whom were screaming and crying. As I pushed my way back through the throng of people somebody grabbed my arm. "How is he, is he badly hurt?" I did not answer but continued to where Paul was.

He covered the child with the blanket and then we both got the stretcher out of the ambulance and loaded the poor lifeless body onto it. There was a huge amount of blood on the road and somebody put a shovel full of earth onto it. We loaded the child into the ambulance and Paul told me to just sit down as there was nothing further to be done.

I was in a state of shock and just could not take in everything that was happening. The doors of the ambulance slammed shut and Paul climbed into the driver's seat. I realized that I was alone in the back of the ambulance with this broken, crushed body that was still dripping blood onto the floor of the ambulance. I shouted to Paul asking him what should I do but he just told me to stay sitting down and mind that I did not slip on the blood that was all over the floor. Every corner that we went round the blood swirled across the floor like a red tide coming in. We went round corners going the opposite way and the tide receded the other way.

In a flash, we arrived at the hospital. Thank God for that I thought. The sooner I can get out of the ambulance and not have to look at that mess again the better. Paul pulled up outside the casualty department and got out of the vehicle. He came to the back of the ambulance, opened one door and told me to get out. I didn't need telling twice. I was out in an instant. He was very calm and asked me if I was all right. I just nodded at him and he said something and then disappeared into the casualty department.

Within seconds, he reappeared accompanied by a doctor and a nurse. All three of them climbed into the back of the ambulance and closed the door behind them. Seconds later they all trooped out again and the doctor and nurse disappeared back into the casualty department. Paul came over to me and offered me a cigarette. I was very conscious of my hands shaking slightly as I took the cigarette from its packet. I felt like a fool. We lit up and stood there savouring the smoke for a few minutes neither of us saying anything.

Suddenly another ambulanceman broke the tranquillity. He looked a real old hand, grey hair and a wrinkled face that looked like an unmade bed. His face had obviously seen death and suffering for years.

"Bad one was it, Paul?" he asked, not giving me a glance.

"Yeah, fatal RTA," Paul replied glumly.

"How old?" the man asked.

"I don't know, maybe nine or ten."

"Bloody hell, poor bastard."

"Yeah, and it's Ron's first 999 call as well."

"Poor bugger," the man said, turning towards me. "Still, don't let it get to you kid. You'll have lots more of these to deal with before you retire. And don't let anybody tell you that you will get used to it. You don't!"

The old hand that day was quite right on both counts. I have unfortunately had to deal with hundreds of fatal incidents since that terrible day, some involving children. And you do not get used to dealing with accidents involving children. Nobody in the Ambulance Service anywhere in the world *gets used to it.*

We finished our cigarettes and I began to wonder why nobody had arrived yet to collect our sad load.

"What do we do now, Paul?" I asked in a very naive way.

"Do? What do you mean do?" he said. "We take the body to the mortuary, get cleaned up and then we will be ready for our next shout."

Oh my God, I thought, not the mortuary again. I had never been inside one of those places until our *decayed, maggot ridden green man* a few days before and it had just not crossed my mind that I would have to go there again so soon.

"Are you OK?" Paul asked. "You look a little green."

"Yes, I think so. I just did not think of all this," I said.

"What do you mean?" Paul asked me in a rather annoyed way.

"Well, I never actually gave death and mortuaries a thought," I told him.

"It's part of the job and if you are going to stay in the Ambulance Service, you had better get used to it," he said. "We spend a great deal of time in mortuaries."

"Come on, then. Let's get down there," Paul quickly said while indicating that I should sit in the front with him. Soon we were heading down to Roberts Street, the address of the Central Mortuary in Manchester.

It was late afternoon and Paul was cursing the build-up of traffic, which was heralding the start of the rush hour. We went through the back streets taking short cuts wherever we could and all too soon we arrived at the mortuary. "Let's go in and see if they are ready for us to bring our body in," said Paul as he climbed out of the ambulance.

As we walked in, the overwhelming stench of disinfectant and carbolic soap rushed into my nostrils. Bloody hell, I thought. What a stink! Fancy having to work in that smell all day.

We were met by a huge man of about forty-five years of age. He had a big round face, which had a strange strained look about it. It's that bloody stink, I thought to myself as I studied his face. No wonder he looks so aggressive. He was dressed in a large full-length rubber apron over his clothes and a pair of white rubber knee length boots adorned his feet.

"Hello Jim," said Paul. "This is my mate, Ron."

"Hello Ron. I don't think I have seen you before," he said. But I was not really listening. I only wanted to get away from the mortuary and leave our pathetic, broken dead child behind.

"Bring it in lads," we were told.

"Come on Ron, Let's get it in, then we can go in for tea." Did he say *tea*? Surely we were not expected to eat after the job we had just done? I caught sight of Paul glaring at me. He must have read my mind but he said nothing.

We unloaded the remains of the child and Paul signed a form. We washed down the stretcher and mopped out the ambulance with some of the vile smelling disinfectant. Finally, it was our turn for a wash and my ordeal at the mortuary was thankfully over. We were back inside the ambulance ready for another job.

"Well, how do you feel now Ron?" Paul said. "It's a pity that you had to start off with such a messy one on your first real shout."

What did he want, I thought? Does he want me to give marks out of ten? I just stared at him not really knowing what to say. I was what today would be called traumatised.

"How can you talk about it as a *messy one?* That was someone's child," I said.

"Listen, I feel as sorry about that kid as you do but he is dead. We have a shitty job to do. We don't go over what if this or what if that or anything else. You had better get used to seeing broken and battered bodies, including kids, or piss off now!"

Paul picked up the radio handset and started to speak to the Control Room.

"Return to station for your meal, base out."

We were on our way back to station for tea. Although I did not feel sick, I certainly could not think about eating anything. I was aware that this was unusual for me since I have a really good appetite.

Ten minutes later, we were getting out of the ambulance in the station. I was shaking slightly and I felt in a daze.

"What have you got to eat, Ron?" Paul asked.

"Oh, I think I have some sandwiches," I said rather absently.

"Well make sure that you eat them — all of them," Paul said. "If you don't eat just because you have had a shitty job, you will not last five minutes around here."

I felt sick as I forced down every mouthful until it was all eaten. Suddenly, the old hand came into the Mess Room and sat down next to me.

"Hello kid, I'm Bill," he said. His face had a thousand lines on it. In fact, his forehead reminded me of the threads on a bolt! He looked about sixty years old. I found out later that he was just forty!

"Hi Bill, I'm Ron," I said.

"Yeah, I know. We met at the M.R.I. (Manchester Royal Infirmary) earlier on," he reminded me. "Don't worry about that shout. It's rough having one like that at any time but especially on your first shout."

I felt that Bill probably understood how new recruits felt after bad jobs, so I confided in him. "I just did not expect to see that sort of thing so soon after starting," I said.

"You were with Paul because you already *had* a First Aid Certificate. *You are trained*!"

"I have not had any training for that type of damage," I said.

"Nobody gets trained for *that*. Your training comes through experience. Paul said that you did well and don't forget, these shitty jobs don't come to order. Welcome to the real world, Ron!"

The rest of the week was much quieter. Just a few minor emergency calls until the last evening of our shift. We started our last shift at 1300 hrs. We went out on routine non-urgent work for the afternoon and returned to station for our meal at about 1700 hrs. I gobbled up my sandwiches and a coffee.

We did a number of simple emergencies after tea and at about 2030 hrs, while we were returning to station, I asked Paul to stop at a Chinese take-away so that I could get a curry. I had to put up with all sorts of comments from him but I was still hungry! We stopped at a good take-away on Birch Street, near to the station and I bought my curry.

We arrived back at station at around 2045 hrs and to my dismay, we were the only crew in the station which meant that we would be the next out! Paul had warned me how risky it was to try to eat when not on an official meal break, but I thought that I knew best.

I had just taken my first mouthful when suddenly my nerves were shattered by the spine chilling noise of the bells! I held my breath as I counted the number of rings, one … two ... three. Oh hell, I thought.

I leapt to my feet and ran out of the Mess Room headed towards the ambulance. As I got in, Paul shouted, "RTA, pedestrian knocked down by a bus, Stockport Road, near the Devonshire Hotel Ardwick."

Paul was quite right. It really was too risky to try to eat except during an official meal break and even then, it was not always possible. Paul was a good driver and as we clanged along the road, people turned to watch us flash past. I suddenly realised that I was actually watching where we were going and I was taking notice of things.

This was a change from my first 999 call. That one had been only a few days ago but it seemed like a lifetime. We charged up Hyde Road and onto Devonshire Street. At the junction of Stockport Road, traffic was at a standstill and as we turned onto Stockport Road, we could see that traffic was now forming a stationary queue behind a double-decker bus. Paul wound his way slowly through the stationary traffic and people who were milling around and brought the ambulance to a stop a few yards in front of the bus.

We both got out of the ambulance at the same time. Paul shouted to me to open the rear doors and drop the step. I did this with lightning speed and then I joined him at the front of the bus.

This was an older type bus, the type that is only seen in museums these days. These buses had a very small driver's cab, a big bonnet and radiator, and an open platform at the rear for passengers to get on and off. The front axle was a steel beam which was fairly close to the ground.

Paul was, in fact, lying under the front of the bus looking at what appeared to be a soggy bundle of rags.

"What do you want me to do?" I asked him.

"Give me a hand to get her from under the axle will you?" he said.

In split second, I was also under the front of the bus and looking at the 'rags' which were just a few inches away from my face. There was a huge pool of blood on the road and it rapidly became obvious that the 'bundle of rags' was in fact an old lady who was lying face down on the road. The axle of the bus was across the small of her back.

"Is she trapped?" I asked.

"No. Look at the space between her back and the axle," he replied. Sure enough, there were quite a few inches of space.

We started to very carefully and slowly ease her out from underneath the bus. As we were getting her out, we realised that she was making some strange sounds, like someone blowing bubbles quietly. We did not have any idea as to the extent of her injuries and I had no idea what the noises were.

"What's that noise, Paul?" I asked rather alarmed.

"Never mind the noise. Let's just get her out," he said.

We finally manoeuvred her out from under the bus. We were then able to start and find out what injuries she had suffered.

"Jesus Christ," Paul said as he turned her over for the first time. Her face was *missing*. There was just a mass of bloody, pulpy tissue all matted together and bleeding profusely. The noises that I heard were bubbles coming through the pulp as she breathed in and out. Strangely, there was steam coming from her warm blood as it leaked out onto the road. That sight fascinated me.

"Well, at least she is breathing." said Paul. "Let's get her into the ambulance. Can you get some help with the stretcher?"

As I stood up, somebody grabbed my arm. "I'm the driver," a voice said. "How is she?"

"She's bad mate," said Paul. "What happened, could you tell us?"

"She just stepped in front of me. I didn't stand a chance. It was not my fault," he insisted.

I dashed off for the stretcher asking a bystander to give me a hand. As I released the stretcher from its fitting, the bystander said, "I know you. Don't you do car repairs? I've seen you when I've taken my car in for a service at the garage. Is this your part-time job?"

I just looked at him. Can you imagine doing this as a part-time job, I thought?

"No, this is what I do for a living. This is my job." I felt a strange sense of pride in saying that, even in the situation that I was in.

As we placed the stretcher on the road next to the old lady, the bus driver was still very distressed. "Will I have to take all the blame?" His question was not really addressed to anybody. It was more for whoever was listening.

"How far did you travel with her under the axle?" Paul asked.

"Oh, I don't know. Probably ten or fifteen yards," he replied.

"Let's get her into the ambulance, Ron. You take the legs and I'll take the top," said Paul. "OK. We will lift on three, one … two … three…" And as if by magic, the bundle was placed onto the stretcher. In a flash, she was in the ambulance.

In the relative light of the ambulance, we could see the terrible mess that the old lady was in. I tried to work out where her nose and her eyes should be.

"Where are her nose and mouth, Paul?" I asked.

"Ten yards behind the bloody bus!" he said quickly. "Hold tight, this is going to be a fast run."

The rear doors slammed shut and in seconds, we were flying along Stockport Road towards Manchester Royal Infirmary. As we bounced and clattered along, I was watching our patient. There was nothing that I could do other than to hang on and hold onto the pulp that was still bubbling away. She was thankfully unconscious when we were at the accident and she was still in the same state as I watched her.

I didn't realise it, but we had actually arrived at MRI casualty. Paul suddenly opened the doors of the ambulance and dropped the step with a thud which startled me. "Is she still with us?" he asked.

"I think so. She's still bubbling."

"OK. Let's get her in quickly," he said. We unloaded the stretcher and its sad load and hurried into the Casualty Department. Paul reported our arrival to the Sister-in-Charge, and suddenly, our patient was surrounded by doctors and other medical staff all starting the fight to try to save her life. They were like a well-oiled machine. It was incredible to watch such a performance.

"Oh no, not you *again*," a doctor said and I realised he was talking to me. But I didn't hear him or register his comment.

All I could hear was a voice in my head, which was saying over and over again: "What are you doing here?" Why I wanted to do this job I do not know. I thought, I really don't think that I can stand this. I was seriously considering leaving the ambulance service and returning to being a motor mechanic. Working in the garage was a dirty job, but by God, it was nothing in comparison to this carnage!

Suddenly there was a tug at my sleeve.

"Are you OK?" It was the doctor again.

"Pardon?" I said.

"You seem a bit of a jinx, don't you?" he said.

"Why do you say that?" I wondered out loud.

"Well, there was the child crushed under the bus a few days ago and now this," the doctor said.

"He is a bloody jinx," said Paul as he returned from washing his hands. "All this during his first week on shifts."

Suddenly the bubbling stopped. The old lady was dead.

Afterwards Paul and I had a long discussion about different calls and as Paul pointed out, they were not all like that last one. Some of the calls could be quite uplifting in a strange way. In fact, that happened on our next night working together.

That next shift was another late shift and it had a surprise for me, but it was not as brutal as my previous few jobs had been.

At 2101, the bells rang: ring, ring, ring. Paul and I had been doing a crossword between us and this was a 'saved by the bells' situation as we were both stuck for the answer to a crossword clue.

Paul went to the ambulance and I collected the pink ticket. It was for a maternity case, and the lady was going to St. Marys Maternity Hospital. I gave Paul the address and he knew where it was. I didn't know so I asked Paul. It was all part of learning the area. Since we worked all over Manchester, there were literally thousands of roads, streets, avenues, crescents, and lanes which we had to learn. This was in fact a new skill. It was called topography.

"Where is Brierley Avenue, Higher Ardwick, Paul?" I asked as we headed out.

"It's near Ardwick Green," said Paul, "You'll recognise it when we get there."

It was a slum clearance area. Some houses were derelict and some were still lived in. Clearly, quite a few were well on the way to being derelict but still lived in.

We pulled into Brierley Avenue but it was difficult to find the house. Most houses did not have numbers or the front doors were missing on the derelict property. Paul spotted a man further down the street waving to us. As we arrived, I jumped out and almost immediately, I heard screaming from inside the house.

"It's the wife. She's bloody having the kid now. Get a move on!" said the man and with that I hustled quickly into the house.

"Watch where you are walking. A lot of floorboards are missing," he cautioned. British houses mostly had wooden floors constructed with floorboards and there was a gap of two or three feet below down to the earth.

"Do you have any lights in the house?" I asked.

"No, the bastards cut off our leckie, because we didn't pay the bill." *So, no electricity.* Another common challenge in these places.

"OK. Where is your wife?" I asked.

"She's in the back room, but most of the boards are missing in there. We had to burn them to keep warm," he said.

What a state the house was in, or should I say *what was left of it*. As I went into the back room, I carefully picked my way on the floorboards that were left. I saw his wife lying on the few boards that were in one piece in the room.

"Hello, I'm the ambulanceman. Are you able to sit up for me, please?" I asked.

"You're a bit young for this job, aren't you? How old are you?" she asked.

"Never mind my age. Let's get you into the ambulance. Can you get up?" I asked again.

"My waters have gone and the sprog is on its way. I'm having it here," she said.

Just then, she let out another blood curdling scream and announced that it was on its way. We had no light and almost no floor to work on.

Her husband had a pan of water on the open fire and when I asked him what it was for he said, "How should I know? You're the bloody ambulance service. You always seem to want boiling water."

"Maybe it is just to keep husbands out of the way and busy while the baby is being born?" I joked but he gave me a look to wither me. Paul had joined me by this time and had brought a torch with him. The flashlight was about as bright as a cigarette end, but it was better than nothing.

Since there was nowhere to work, Paul suggested that I jump down onto the earth below the floor level. His advice was a great help since it gave me some room to work. I stood to one side expecting Paul to join me but he didn't. I was in at the deep end in more ways than one since this was going to be my first delivery!

"Tell me if you need help, Ron. I know you have done a few deliveries before." That last comment was for the patient's benefit in order to give her confidence in my ability. I was flying by the seat of my pants on this one, but no need for her to know that.

"I've sent for the midwife. She should be here shortly," we were told.

"Can you get me a couple of blankets, Paul? I don't want the baby landing on any dirt," I said.

He handed them over, and I lay the blankets down and positioned myself so that I could deliver the baby safely, making sure that it did not drop down towards the earth floor.

Then in a big rush, with no real warning, the baby arrived. I was caught unawares as to how slippery it was, never having done this before, but I got a good grip and almost immediately, it started crying.

"What is it?" asked the dad. "Is it a boy or a girl?"

"A boy and he has good lungs. What a noise he's making."

"That's five boys and one girl now," said the husband.

"That's how I knew it was on the way. You get to know when you've had a few," said the mother.

The baby was wrapped in a blanket and placed next to the mother by the time the midwife arrived a couple of minutes later. She asked us if everything was OK.

"He delivered the baby," said Paul pointing at me.

"Well done, how many have you done now?" she said smiling at me.

In a whisper, I told her that it was my first and she congratulated me again adding, "I thought you probably had not done many. You're too young."

We waited outside and eventually the midwife asked us to move the mother and baby to the hospital.

We loaded our priceless cargo and headed for the maternity hospital which was about two miles away. As we were unloading both patients at the hospital, the mother thanked me for delivering her baby safely and she asked me my name.

"My name is Ron. Why?"

"I was going to call my baby after you, but I am looking for a religious name and Ron is not religious," she continued. "What's your mate's name?"

"Paul, he's called Paul," I said.

"That will do. He is going to be called Paul."

After cleaning up and getting washed ourselves, we called Control.

We finally arrived back on station at 2314, more than two hours after our normal finishing time but I did not mind. It was a very happy shift and I really enjoyed it. It was a real learning experience, not only where Brierley Avenue was, but how to deliver a baby!

I thought to myself, now, if only we could have a few more days like this, it would be fantastic. I had countless days like that for the next thirty years, where things turned out well rather than for the worst. And I would eventually deliver a total of fourteen healthy babies, including two sets of twins before I retired.

4. Brawn and Brains - Training School

It turned out that organised training for ambulance staff was virtually non-existent in most services right up until the late 1960s. As a result, the standards of treatment varied dramatically from authority to authority. There were strong attitudes about the need for further training and one of the most common ones was: "We've always done it this way. *Why change now?*" In other words, although procedures had not changed for twenty to thirty years, it did not mean that the process for treating casualties was good enough. I came across a lot of obstruction to change over the years, particularly by the senior crew members.

However, change was on its way in spite of them, and I was glad. Once organised training was formally introduced, the ambulance service would never be the same again!

One of the main starting points in the UK happened about 1966. The National Health Service (NHS), which was the government body that was responsible for all aspects of public health care, announced the findings of the *Miller Report*. This document set out the future national standards of patient care and outlined new training for ambulance staff which was called, at that time, *para-medical training.*

In Manchester, this training was first implemented in 1968 and took the form of residential training courses of varying lengths. This training was delivered at approved Ambulance Service Training Schools located in various parts of the country. If by a given date, an individual had gained more than two years' service time but less than five years, then he was required to attend a two-week residential course at a designated Training School. If it was less than two years' service by the named date, then a person had to attend a six-week residential course.

If you were a real 'old timer' with more than five years' service then you were exempt until everybody else had attended their designated courses. This effectively meant that most of the men with seniority would not attend any formal training for years to come. And it was mainly this group who did not want the changes anyway. This naturally pitted *us* against *them* and it caused quite a bit of friction.

Lots of the newer ambulancemen embraced the new training. For the first time in the UK, successful completion of your course would give ambulance personnel a nationally recognised qualification as a "QAM" or "Qualified Ambulanceman" — and not a *First Aider*. There were virtually no women working in the ambulance service in those days although Manchester had about ten ladies who did out-patient work only. They had in fact joined the Ambulance Service during World War II and some were nearing retirement age.

Years of study by the government had brought in the training program and along with it, a recommendation for improved equipment. By the time my turn came to attend Training School in May 1969, I had completed just two years' service. I wanted to go to the Training School so I asked to be sent on the two-week course. I was actually two weeks over my "two year service" mark and as such, I was really looking forward to the two-week course. I was settled and had my own permanent crewmate but I wanted the chance to improve my standard of patient care. Reluctantly, my senior officer approved my request.

I had been crewed up with a Shift Leader Bill Stone some months before. He was a nice chap, about 40 years of age. He was very polite and quiet but looked on us *younger enders*, as he called us, with complete bewilderment. We, the *younger end,* wanted as much training as we could get and my own view was really one of frustration. I wanted as much advanced training as soon as I could get it but advanced training was also new and only in its infancy.

When I had been an auxiliary fireman, I participated in training and drills that were viewed as compulsory because practicing such activities instilled a 'second nature' response at incidents. Yet with the ambulance services, where we were in a job where we were trying to save lives, some members of staff still frowned on taking further training.

I was very happy when I officially received my joining instructions to attend a two-week course for the first two weeks in May 1969. The course was to be held at the Cheshire Ambulance Service Training School, Wrenbury Hall near Nantwich, Cheshire. Nantwich was a small town over a thousand years old located about fifty miles southwest of Manchester. Wrenbury Hall was a palatial old country mansion that was used by Cheshire Ambulance Service as their Training School. It was located in a beautiful countryside setting just a few miles outside Nantwich.

The course was residential and full uniform was to be worn at all times during the day. I was very excited and really looking forward to the course. I discussed the course with Bill, my crewmate but really he did not show very much interest. "Go and see what it's all about and let them know how we do things here in Manchester," is all he would say.

I arrived at Wrenbury Hall on Sunday evening at about 1800 hrs. I had travelled with a colleague who worked at the same station as I did and we had almost the same length of service. There were other ambulancemen there from all over the country including Northern Ireland. Some were in "civvies" and others were in uniform. After a short time an officer appeared and introduced himself as Mr. Graham. He was dressed in full uniform with rank markings on his epaulettes. He told us that he was the Duty Officer which seemed very *military*. We did not really have actual officers in Manchester, just civilians who had officer titles, so this was a novelty to me.

Mr. Graham gave the proceedings an air of efficiency. As our names were called out, we were given a key to our rooms and each of us had our own room. We were also given various forms to complete. The residential block was a short walk away down the main driveway and we all went off to find our rooms and unpack our belongings. We were there for two weeks with a trip home during the middle weekend.

We were there to learn some new skills with which to improve the standard of patient care. Words like *skills* and terms like *patient care* are in common usage today but back in the ambulance service of the 1960s and 1970s, these were the new buzz words which conjured up all kinds of thoughts.

Did it mean that since we were going to learn *skills*, then we must be *unskilled* at the moment, no good at what we did? Or did it mean we had no finesse? We would soon find out.

The rest of Sunday evening was spent checking things like fire exits and assembly points, the location of lecture theatres, meal times, and of course locating and sampling the fare at the nearest pub. After a really good night out at the Cotton Tree Pub, the small group of us wandered back and typical of young men who had just consumed a few beers, we then wanted food.

Fortunately Wrenbury Hall must have had the likes of us there before because there was an enormous lump of Cheshire cheese left out for us in the dining room, alongside an ample supply of bread, butter and pickled onions. It was heaven. We ate our fill, told jokes and eventually we all went off to bed. We nominated one ex-army lad to make sure that everybody was awake at 0700 hrs. He got the job because he claimed never to need a clock for waking up! We would see.

No sooner had I gone to bed or so it seemed than there was a loud knocking at my door accompanied by shouting, "Come on, get up, it's seven o'clock. Get out of bed!"

"OK I'm up," I shouted. I was out of bed in seconds and after a nice warm shower, I was wide-awake. I was also very eager to start the course. I got dressed in my uniform, which I had pressed specially for the course, and as I checked myself over in the long mirror on the wall, I actually thought smugly how smart I looked.

I went down to the main building and into the lounge. There were already some people in the lounge reading newspapers. They all had one thing in common. They were all in uniform and they all had "pips" (rank markings) on their shoulders. These were all officers! I mumbled a few 'good mornings' but nobody seemed to notice me or so I thought. It had the air of being in a doctor's surgery.

Suddenly, in a voice that would not have been out of place on a military parade ground, a voice boomed out, "Is you head cold, laddie?" I looked around to see who he was shouting at, but there was nobody else behind me.

"You, is your bloody head cold?" The owner of the voice looked brutal in my fairly naive eyes. He was a big, middle-aged man with slicked back black hair that reminded me of patent leather.

"Err, no Sir," I mumbled uncomfortably. I noticed that some of the other pips had put down their newspapers and were now watching me. I was extremely embarrassed as more and more eyes looked in my direction.

"Well, take your bloody cap off when you are inside," he bellowed again, this time making himself abundantly clear. My reflexes kicked in and it was removed in the blink of an eye!

"Sorry, Sir, but I thought that I had to wear it at all times," I said.

The officer stood up and started to walk towards me. Everybody was watching me now, even some other ambulancemen who had wandered in during the exchange of words.

"What's your name and where are you from?" His face was set like granite.

"Gillatt, Sir. I'm from Manchester City Ambulance Service."

"Well son, you don't *think* until you are told to. You are here to do as you are told and to learn. *We* will tell you when to think. Got it?"

"Yes, Sir. Sorry." I could feel myself going purple with embarrassment and I just wished that I were somewhere else at that moment.

This was a terrible blow. The last thing that I wanted was to start off on the wrong foot. I felt sure now that I was a *marked man* for the rest of the course. I was to find out just how *marked* I was on the last day of the course. Fortunately at that moment, I was saved by the bell. It was ringing to announce breakfast. As the officers walked past me on their way into the dining room, they all gave me a sideways, belittling look which made me feel more embarrassed. The rest of us *other ranks* then went into the dining room and formed an orderly queue for our first meal at Training School.

During breakfast, I noticed that all the officers were sitting at a long table, which was on a slightly raised section of the floor. This was obviously to give them a complete view of the dining room. It seemed very intimidating. I still felt very embarrassed about being chastised over wearing my cap. Suddenly, there was a loud knocking from the officers' table. A hush fell over the dining room and everybody turned to look in the direction of the knocking.

"Good morning gentlemen. When you have finished your breakfast, go straight to the lounge and sit down. If you don't know where the lounge is, Mr. Gillatt from Manchester will show you. Where are you, Mr. Gillatt?"

I was feeling bright red in the face with embarrassment as I put my hand up. This reminded me of being back at school. "I can't see you. Stand up will you." Bastard, I thought, he's just trying to humiliate me. I stood up to loud jeers and cheers from the lads on the course. The lads on my table made various comments about the officer, including doubts about his parentage! I suddenly noticed that the officer was smiling "OK, mate, thanks," he said with a smile. Maybe he was not as aggressive as he seemed.

I sat down and finished my coffee. The lads at the table made the usual type of comments about how *well in* I must be if he knew my name and we had a good laugh. I needed cheering up at that moment. I told them the cap story and to my amazement, their attitude changed towards the officer. I was given advice on how to handle him in the future, things like, "Tell him to piss off. This isn't the bloody army," and "Report the bastard to the commandant." We had not seen the commandant yet, only heard about him.

We all took our seats in the lounge and after a couple of minutes, all the officers walked in and sat down on a long row of chairs at the front of the room. The hum of the lads talking slowly died down until there was silence. You could hear a pin drop. "All stand," and like robots, we all stood up. We had no idea why.

Then into the room came a short, well-built man in his late forties. He had a jovial face and his hair had been blond but was now mixed with a lot of grey. He was in uniform and on his shoulders were rank markings consisting of a laurel wreath and two pips. He walked up to a lectern and stood there for a few seconds surveying the assembled pupils. "All sit," boomed the voice again and like obedient dogs, we all sat down.

"Good morning, gentlemen. My name is Mr. Andrews. I am the commandant here at Wrenbury Hall and I welcome you to the Cheshire Ambulance Service Training School."

So this was the big cheese, I thought.

"I don't know you and you don't know me," he continued. "Let's find out about you all. We shall hear from you all in turn so we can find out who *you* are, where you are from and why you are in the ambulance service. We will start with you."

The commandant pointed to a lad on the front row. He introduced himself as Jack Watson and he was from City of Derby Ambulance Service. He had been in the service for just under two years and he had previously worked as a fitter at Rolls Royce.

I listened with interest to all the lads as they each gave a potted history of themselves, which services they were from and a little bit about their backgrounds. Finally, it was my turn and I introduced myself: "Ron Gillatt from Manchester City Ambulance Service."

"Ah, yes, Mister Ron Gillatt, the chap with the cold head," said the commandant. There was a lot of jeering from the rest of the lads. As I could feel myself getting more and more embarrassed yet again, I thought, *enough is enough.*

"Sir, I did not have a cold head. I was trying to follow exactly the printed instructions that were issued to me. They say that full uniform will be worn at *all* times."

There was an uncomfortable pause, a general shuffling of chairs and a few little coughs.

"Well, so we will have to teach you to read as well will we, Mister Gillatt? The instructions that you were issued with did not say that at all," said the commandant. I was starting to feel very nervous about speaking out when suddenly a chap stood up two rows in front of me.

He was holding a sheet of paper in his hand. "Sir, this is the instruction sheet that we received and it states that full uniform will be worn at *all* times. "

The commandant motioned to one of his officers to get the paper from the ambulanceman who was by now grinning at me. The officer took the paper and handed it over. The commandant read over it in silence. Finally he announced: "It would seem that our instructions should be made clearer. Let me say that caps must not be worn inside the buildings. Please disregard these written instructions. Please accept our apologies, Ron."

I finished doing my introduction and sat down. I was quivering slightly with nerves. I had actually challenged the top brass and I had won! This was not something that I had done very often before. I had stood up for myself in front of fifty other people and the commandant had called me by my first name!

When all the introductions had been completed, the instructors took over and outlined the contents of the course. It was spread over two weeks and there would be frequent assessments. There were 101 things that were thought necessary for us students to know. We were then introduced to all the instructors and we were all allocated to *syndicates* or groups that we would remain in for the duration of the course. I was in red syndicate and our instructor would be Mr. Graham assisted by a trainee instructor, Mr. Eric Wardley.

We were eventually led away by our instructor and we were taken to our syndicate room or training room. We were issued with some very basic training manuals and some other paperwork and that was the start of the course.

The first week passed very quickly. There were written assessments before and after each training session. We were also required to do practical assessments. Most of the equipment was new to me coming from a service which had virtually no equipment at all. Compared to us, Cheshire Ambulance Service was outstandingly well-equipped with all kinds of sophisticated kit.

It was during that first week that I thought how good it would be to work for a service like Cheshire. They were a really go-ahead service with things like the *Minuteman* which was an an oxygen-driven resuscitator. They had Oro-pharyngeal Airways, burns kits, very well fitted out dressing boxes and even a Rescue Kit. What luxury!

All the practical training sessions were simulated emergencies and were carried out around the grounds or in outbuildings and even in the dormitory block. They were made as realistic as possible using imitation wounds and plastic injuries with what seemed like gallons of stage blood!

On the Friday morning of our first week, we were given an exam, which covered everything that we had done during the first week of the course. The written paper covered Anatomy and Physiology of all the different body systems. There were also separate papers on Resuscitation, Burns, Head and Spinal injuries and Emergency Childbirth.

We were asked about the advanced equipment that we had been training on and we also had practical assessments. These involved the individual ambulanceman being given a number of simulated incidents to deal with. The patient was made up using stage make-up and a number of false injuries were also added. The instructor would then point out that any available equipment could be used and a time limit was placed on dealing with the incident.

The rest was then up to the poor ambulanceman to do his best and hopefully at a standard that was acceptable by the instructor.

At last, all the written, oral and practical assessments were over. We were then called in one-by-one to be interviewed by Mr. Andrews, the commandant. I was about number six and in due course, my turn came. I knocked on his door and walked in.

"Good afternoon, Ron, sit down please." I could see that he was reading my exam papers and scribbling various comments on the different pages.

"How are you finding the course?" he asked.

"I think it is great, I am enjoying it very much thanks."

"Well, you seem to be doing very well indeed. No problems with anything?" he said.

"No, I am really enjoying everything about the course. I particularly enjoy working with such good equipment. You seem to have everything in Cheshire," I told him.

He looked puzzled by my comment. "Do you not have similar equipment in Manchester?"

"We don't really have anything. Just a couple of blankets, an oxygen cylinder and one or two other bits," I answered.

Mr. Andrews gave me a long look and then said, "Maybe you should transfer to Cheshire County, ever thought about that?"

"Err, no Sir, I have not. I don't even know where the Cheshire boundary is at its nearest point to where I live."

"Where do you live?" asked Mr. Andrews and I told him that I lived in Burnage, Manchester.

Mr. Andrews had never heard of *Burnage* but he started to mention places in Cheshire where there was an Ambulance Station. "Are you anywhere near Macclesfield, Dukenfield, Knutsford, Altrincham, or Cheadle Hulme?"

"I am not that far away from Cheadle Hulme, maybe seven or eight miles?" I interrupted his flow. "Isn't it Cheadle Hulme where that train crashed a couple of years ago?"

"You are referring to the Lollipop Special," he said.

"Yes, that's it. I went up on the evening of the crash to have a look at the damage."

"Well, it sounds as though Cheadle Hulme is your nearest Cheshire County Ambulance Station. How about it Ron? Do you think you would like to work for us?" I was nervous at the prospect of transferring to such a service.

"Are there any vacancies at Cheadle Hulme, Mr. Andrews?" I asked politely.

"Well, I will tell you what. Why don't you go and have a look at the station over the weekend and I will try to find out about manning requirements." I thanked Mr. Andrews and left his office.

I collected all my kit from my room and my colleague and I left to go home for the weekend. I was very excited about the visit that I was planning to make to Cheadle Hulme Ambulance Station over the weekend. I was not sure if I knew anybody who worked there. We were always talking to crews from different areas but we would not know which station they were from, only which authority they were working with. We knew that by the badge on their uniforms.

We had also been set a lot of homework for the weekend. Things like anatomy, physiology, signs and symptoms of injuries and medical conditions and a whole host of related stuff. We were going to have an exam first thing on Monday morning as we started the second week and I wanted to continue to do well. They will not want me in Cheshire if I am not good enough I thought.

Suddenly I realised that I actually *wanted* to work for Cheshire County Ambulance Service. This was no longer just *maybe*. This was now *definitely*. I felt elated that the commandant of the Training School had actually asked me if I had considered working for them. To me, it was like he was offering me a job!

I spent the weekend doing a lot of studying and I must admit that even though it was very in-depth, I really enjoyed the subjects. I was thoroughly enjoying myself.

On Sunday morning, I decided to take a break from studying so I went off to Cheadle Hulme to try to find the Ambulance Station. I had to look at the map to find it and I arrived at about 1000 hrs. As I drove into the station car park, I noticed a number of ambulances in various stages of being cleaned. All the equipment was stripped out and placed on top of the stretcher cots.

I could see that in Cheshire, they had actual stretchers with wheels. They were designed to be wheeled, unlike ours in Manchester which had to be carried. There seemed to be mountains of kit and it was all neatly stacked on the trolleys. There was a group of five men involved in the cleaning and as I drove in, they stopped what they were doing and looked in my direction.

I parked my car and got out. As I walked over to them, one of them, a man of about fifty, slim and very rugged looking came towards me. His uniform had a pip on each shoulder and he wore a white shirt. This must be an officer I thought.

"Morning Sir, can I help you?" he asked.

"My name is Ron Gillatt, Sir. I have just come to have a look at the station if that is alright." He looked puzzled, as if he needed more information.

"How do you mean?" he asked.

"Well, I work for Manchester Ambulance and I am at Wrenbury Hall at the moment on a two-week course. The boss, Mr. Andrews said that I should come and have a look at the nearest Cheshire station to where I live. That's why I am here. I don't want to be in the way."

"My name's Mike Jones. I am one of the Sub-Officers," he said holding out his hand.

We shook hands and he immediately turned to the other men and shouted, "Hey, Andrews has sent him from Wrenbury to see what a proper station looks like. What did you say your name was?"

"It's Ron Gillatt, Mr. Jones" I repeated.

"Bloody hell. Don't call me *Mister*. Everybody calls me Mick." Mick turned to his lads and introduced me to them. "This is Ron. He works for The Binmen!"

I looked at him wondering what he had meant by *The Binmen*. He could see my expression and quickly clarified what he was talking about.

"The Binmen is the name that everybody calls Manchester Ambulance Service. You know, like the dustbin men that collect garbage: pick 'em up, chuck 'em in and piss off with them! We see ambulancemen from all over and the treatment given varies dramatically," he said. "Manchester ambulancemen are known as the *Binmen,* Derbyshire lads are known as the *Hillbillies*. Didn't you know that? Each service does its best for training but some are better than others."

Conceited bastard, I thought. How dare he imply that we don't do a good job. He could see I wasn't very pleased.

"I don't mean to insult anybody, but you're just not given the training that we get. That's what I mean," he explained quickly and then changed the subject. "Do you fancy a brew?" he asked.

The other men came over and I was introduced to them. They were Arnold Jackson, Philip Brown, John Strines and Ray Black. They formed two crews and Mick stayed at the station. His duty was to deal with the general running of the station itself.

To my surprise, there was a Control Room in the station. I was given a tour of the station, which finished in what I considered to be a "space-age" Control Room when compared with the one that I was used to at Belle Vue in Manchester. This Control Room covered the east part of Cheshire County which is a large county area with lots of farming, industry, and a number of cities. I could imagine there was the potential for a great variety of calls. East and West Cheshire were divided by the M6 motorway which ran north and south through the centre of the county. The West Cheshire area was controlled by another Control Room located

THE GREEN MAN | TRUE STORIES OF A PARAMEDIC FROM THE ROADSIDE

in Chester which was the main city in Cheshire.

The controllers had headsets on and it seem incredibly efficient and also most of the time very quiet. This was because the room was sound proofed with sound-deadening panels on the walls.

"Brews ready," somebody shouted and I was ushered into the Mess Room. This was a little bit like a small dining room with a long table and chairs round it. There was also a small kitchen and the one thing that stood out to me was how clean it all was.

We sat down and the general discussion was about Wrenbury and the training course. I found out that the national two-week course that I was on had been greatly influenced by Cheshire, as it had been their standard basic course for the last few years. No wonder Mick had made the comment about their training and ours. I was beginning to feel quite inferior to these men who clearly were receiving far better training than we were.

The lads made me feel very welcome and made it clear that they did not look on Manchester ambulancemen as being bad at their jobs. They felt that we deserved better training. I agreed with this sentiment and pointed out that the National Training Program was now becoming well established.

"Yeah, but what about the old farts?" asked Philip.

"What do you mean?" I said.

"What training are the older men having?" he asked.

"Well, they don't have to go on a course. They are considered to be good at their jobs already. They have got the experience. We have not." I knew that was the government ruling, but these guys had their own opinions and were not shy about expressing them.

"That's bollocks! Half of them have been at it since the war. They are not up to date on the newer methods of treating people and most don't have any interest in changing."

I thought about that for a moment and suddenly realised that what they were saying was right. The old timers teach all us newer blokes. Whatever they did, right or wrong, is what we were taught. As *we* become the *old farts* we were still passing on old methods. But that was only because they didn't know any better and were not given the chance to learn the new ways yet. Now that we were taking training courses to teach us the correct way to do things, we would have to find a way to get the *old timers* to adapt to the modern methods. Not much hope of that, I thought. When I thought about it, they should have sent the older blokes *first* or sent regular crews together.

In Manchester, we had permanent partners. I worked with Bill Stone who fell into the old-timer slot. He had been with the Ambulance Service for many years and although his attitude to patients was superb, he had not had the opportunity to go on any training courses. In his day, there were none to take. It occurred to me that maybe it was time that we *newer* blokes should start to train the *older* blokes in the methods that we were being taught at Training School. I wasn't sure Bill would be much of a fan of me if I started telling him how to do things.

Meanwhile, the conversation with the lads at Cheadle Hulme soon turned to the type of work that they did. They covered a very different type of area compared to the one I was used to in Manchester. They had a lot of countryside and farms, plus the Manchester Airport, the Woodford Airfield and some very fast trunk roads and motorways. They were used to dealing with road accidents involving high speed, whereas we were more accustomed to pedestrian accidents.

In Cheadle Hulme, they also had great distances to travel. In Manchester, we could do a 999 call, pick up the patient, go to the hospital and return to station and we would cover only five or six miles. At Cheadle Hulme, they told me that the average mileage for each job was fifteen to twenty miles. "We have our patients in the ambulance for a long time, so you have to know your stuff when travelling those kind of distances," said Arnold. Yes, that made sense. The longer the patient is in your care, the greater the risk of the patient deteriorating. If you know what you are doing, the patient will probably arrive at hospital in a better condition than when you picked them up. That was the aim of the new advanced training courses.

"Do you fancy working on a county station?" Mick asked me.

"Well, I am hoping to find a vacancy in the Cheshire Service as near home as possible," I said. "I live in Burnage."

His friend Ray spoke up. "I know where that is. This station would be just right for you. Only about eight miles from home," he said. "You should try and get one of the vacancies that we have here if you are interested. But you will have to hurry. Everybody wants to come here you know. It's a very posh area to work."

"I didn't know that there were any vacancies," I said.

"We have two," said Mick. "Tell Andrews on Monday that you want one."

When I finally said my goodbyes and left the station, I had the feeling as I drove back home that I had finally found the place that I really wanted to work.

I returned to Wrenbury Hall after tea on Sunday and unpacked my kit in my room. A few of the other lads had already arrived back and we decided to go for a couple of pints at the Cotton Tree before they closed. Most of us had been doing a lot of studying all weekend and we felt that we were well on top of the work. We had a good laugh in the Cotton Tree pub and after having finished our drinks, we ambled along the inky black lane back to Wrenbury Hall. After arranging with one of the Derby ambulance lads to act as an alarm clock and wake everybody up in the morning, we went to bed.

When we queued up for our breakfast, just as I was sitting down to eat, one of the officers came over to our table.

"Morning lads. How are things this morning then?" It was an officer called Jimmy Richards. He was one of the smartest dressed people that I had ever cast eyes on. The creases in his sleeves and in his trousers looked like knife blades and you could literally see your face in his bulled boots, they were so shiny. He stood about six feet tall, aged about fifty-two or three, and he had a small military-type moustache.

"Which one of you is Ron Gillatt?" he said. Oh no, I thought, not again.

"I am sir," I said as I stood up.

He immediately thrust out his hand and as we started to shake hands he said, "Pleased to meet you kid. I hear that you were looking round my old office yesterday!"

I must have looked puzzled because he then clarified what he meant.

"Didn't you go and see Mick and the lads yesterday?"

"Oh, yes I did," I said, finally figuring out what he meant.

"Good lad that Mick. He took over from me when I came here. I was the Sub Officer there until I was promoted to T.O." he explained, and I knew T.O. meant Training Officer. He continued on. "That's a great station to work from. You get some really shitty jobs, but there's lots of serious stuff too. Plenty to get your teeth into! I am seeing Mr. Andrews this morning. Shall I mention it?"

"Er, no thanks, sir. I will see him myself later," I said.

"OK kid. Best of luck!" said Jimmy as he left.

"What was all that about, Ron?" said Walt from Derby.

"Oh, I called at one of Cheshire stations yesterday just to compare it with one of ours," I explained.

"They don't keep secrets in Cheshire, do they?" said someone else.

"Well, you heard what Mr. Richards was saying. Apparently, he used to be at that station before he came here," I pointed out. "Seems like somebody that I saw there yesterday rung him up or something. I don't know."

We finished our breakfast and slowly walked over to the training room. There were other lads there already and a few of us chatted about the weekend before the dreaded exam. Our T.O. Mr. Graham arrived and had a chat with us until it was time to start work. We filed into the classroom and settled down for the exam. Mr. Graham outlined the rules of the exam: no talking, no notebooks on the desk, keep your nose down. It was just like being back at school! We were given half an hour for the exam and when we had finished, we were to hand our papers in and go outside until everybody had completed it.

The exam paper was quite easy and covered more or less everything that we had done over the previous week. There were a lot of advanced anatomy and physiology questions. We also had to go through lists of signs and symptoms of injuries and illnesses and from those, we had to make a diagnosis. If you had studied properly, it was not difficult, but it made you think.

I finished well within the time, read through the answers that I had given, handed my paper in and went outside. Some other lads had finished before me and of course, the conversation turned to what answers had we had written to different questions. This of course led to debate and then varying degrees of doubt! Finally, everybody was done, and we started into the second week of training.

By this time, the course had become very intensive and covered a whole host of things that ranged all the way from how to take a patient off a home-based renal dialysis machine to map reading! We did a great many practical exercises during the second week and there seemed to be this one chap who was always there to act the part of *the patient*. His name was Noel Watson and I think that he was an ambulanceman at Northwich Ambulance Station, which was one of Cheshire's stations.

Noel was a big lad, about six foot and probably weighed about six-teen stone (225 lbs). He played his part well. He was given the job of simulating a particular condition or injury and we were given a general brief of *the situation* and we then had to deal with it as if it was real.

I was teamed up with a lad from Derbyshire Ambulance Service and at one point, the brief we were given was that that we were a crew attending a *farm accident*. That was it! They gave us no other information other than to point out that two assessors would be watching us carefully and marking us on our performance. Since we were working outside and there were plenty of old building around the grounds, it was quite a realistic setting.

My partner was a lad called Bill or "Willy" as he preferred. We were shown a huge pile of equipment, most of which neither of us had ever seen before, and we were told that this was the ambulance. Anything that we needed to use was on that pile and we were to select whatever we needed to complete the job in a satisfactory way. Finally, we were told that our patient had fallen down an inspection pit in one of the buildings and in doing so, he had fractured a femur and sustained a head injury. Willy and I were asked if we were ready and when we said yes, we were told, "Go!"

We had decided that since Willy was much taller than I was (he was a full six foot three), he would go down into the pit and that I would fetch and carry the gear. Willy, being from Derbyshire, was used to doing things his way and he knew all the equipment that they carried. As for me, I was used to doing things in my own way with virtually no equipment. Then we found that some of the equipment that was available to us, neither of us had ever seen and we did not know how it worked. We were quite the pair. It was like the-blind-leading-the-blind!

So suddenly, there we were with masses of kit and neither of us knowing which way to do the job. It was bloody chaos! Nonetheless, we worked well as a team and very quickly established which leg was injured and the level of head injury. Willy had gone into the pit as arranged and each time he asked for equipment, I passed it to him. Finally, I went down into the pit to help immobilise our patient's injuries and generally help Willy.

When it came to getting the patient out of the pit, we decided that we needed either another crew to help or we would send for the Fire Service. The assessors nearly became *apoplectic* at these suggestions! "You want what?!" one of them yelled at us.

I tried to explain that if it was possible with a real incident like this, we would ask for another crew to help or we would ask for the Fire Service.

Not the answer they wanted, as I soon found out. "The bloody Fire Service put out fires," he bellowed. "Ambulancemen treat and move casualties. *Now get him moved!"*

"Sir, he's too heavy for just the two of us. Can we have some help?"

"Get him moved, now!" screamed the assessor.

Shit, I thought. This is going to be impossible. How could two people of such vastly differing heights, ever possibly lift this giant out of the pit and not aggravate his injuries? It was an impossible task, but we worked as a team and we did our best to produce a good result. In the end, however, we were unable to get Noel out of that pit and we had to concede defeat.

Willy helped me out of the pit and then he hopped out as though it was just a little hole in the ground instead of an open tomb. Noel stayed put. The assessors were becoming irate and threatening to have us sacked for such a disgusting display. Willy and I had to stand there while these two assessors gave us the dressing down of our lives. We thought that we had done a good job, but it seemed that they did not!

As our reprimand was coming to an end and with Noel still trussed up in the pit, Mr. Graham appeared.

"Well, how did they do?" he asked. The assessors repeated their observations to Mr. Graham who by now had walked over to the pit and was peering down at Noel.

Mr. Graham took a long look at Noel and although we could not hear what was being said, it was obvious Mr. Graham was asking Noel about how he had been treated.

"Can I have a word with you gentlemen?" Mr. Graham said to the two assessors. "Ron and Willy, go for a cigarette for five minutes please."

We did not need to be told twice.

We never did find out what went on between Mr. Graham and the assessors, but we did not see them again! By the time we had returned after our cigarettes, they were gone and Mr. Graham had taken over the assessment process. Mr. Graham de-briefed us on our incident and made various points about the way that we had dealt with the job. On the whole, we got a good report.

As we walked back to the classroom, Mr. Andrews appeared from around a corner.

"Mr. Gillatt," he shouted, "Please can I just have a word?"

"Bloody popular with the officers, you are," Willy muttered under his breath as he walked on ahead.

"Ron, I believe that you called at Cheadle Hulme this weekend."

"Yes sir I did."

"How about it then? What did you think?" he asked.

"I thought it was fantastic," I told him. "It is exactly what I am looking for. Nice lads, nice station, nice area and from what Mr. Richards was telling me, plenty of good jobs."

"I have had a word with Mr. Mitchell, the Area Officer and he will keep a vacancy for you until after your final exams on Friday," Mr. Andrews explained. "If you have done well, he has guaranteed you an interview and of course, then it's all up to you."

"Thanks very much, Mr. Andrews. I will try my hardest to do well on Friday, thanks."

I was nearly bursting with pride as I walked to the training room and as I opened the door, there was loud jeering from the rest of the lads in my group. There were the usual comments calling me a creep and a teacher's pet and a few other things, but I really did not care. I wanted that job at Cheadle Hulme, and I was going to do my best to get it.

The rest of the week passed very quickly and was a mixture of theory and plenty of practical stuff. Then, it was Friday, the big day! We spent all morning doing the theory exams and immediately after lunch, we assembled in the main lecture theatre where we were briefed on the afternoon's proceedings. We were given a tag with a number on it. My tag had a "4" on it. This was the order in which we were going to have to complete our practical assessments.

There were teams of Training Officers marking the theory papers and then other Training Officers who were going to conduct the practical assessments. It was very efficient. First, all the theory results were announced on a personal basis. A hush fell over the room and as each person's name was called out, that person made their way to the front where they were given a piece of paper with their overall marks on it.

"Gillatt, R.B.A. Manchester," the Training Officer shouted and in a second I was on my way to the front. Mr. Andrews was handing out the slips of paper and as I arrived to collect mine, he had a huge grin on his face as he handed me the paper.

"Very well done. Just do as well on your practical assessment later," he said in a hushed voice.

I turned to go back to my seat and I glanced down at the paper. My overall theory mark for the course was 98%. I was astounded but very pleased with myself. Eventually, everybody had their marks and sadly, five people had failed. Those poor sods were taken to one side and had their results discussed with the TOs. Then they packed their kit and left.

Then it was time for the practical assessments and since there were five different assessors working at the same time, the first five of us stepped forward. We were all given the same scenario that's how I was one of the first ones to get assessed. My scenario was a patient who had collapsed while connected to their home-based renal dialysis machine. This patient had collapsed as a result of an air embolism and I was the ambulanceman who had been called to attend.

The entire assessment had to be conducted with me giving a running commentary on everything that I was doing, why I was doing it and also answering a barrage of questions from the assessor during the assessment. Suddenly it was all over! Time had flown by and I had now completed not only my practical assessment but also the entire two-week course. I was given my final assessment and told to report to the main lecture theatre to await my final interview with Mr. Andrews.

"Ron Gillatt, please," a voice shouted from outside the slightly open door. It's like being at the doctor's office I thought. I jumped up and made my way to the office. I knocked and waited a moment.

"Come and sit down, Ron. Well, that's the end of your course. Are you glad or sorry?" he said.

"Actually, I am sorry," I said honestly.

"Why are you sorry?"

"Well, I have met some very nice people and I have seen a completely different side of the Ambulance Service to that which I am used to," I explained. "I have also learnt so much in such a short time, I wonder how much more I could learn if I was here for longer."

"As for how much you have taken in, your assessments could not be much better," he told me. "98% overall on the theory and an exceptionally good assessment for your practical. Well done. Now, what about your interview for Cheadle Hulme. Are you available on Monday?" he asked.

"Yes, but only the morning. I start work at 1300 hrs."

"At 1300? What shift is that?" he asked.

"It's called lates — 1300 hrs until 2200 hrs."

"Sounds very anti-social to me. Let me ring Mr. Mitchell." With that, Mr. Andrews phoned Cheadle Hulme to arrange my interview for Monday morning. As I sat there I realised that I was going for an interview for a job that I had not even applied for.

"Hello Fred. George Andrews here at Wrenbury. How are you? Listen Fred, I have the lad from Manchester with me that I was telling you about," he said. "Can you have a chat with him on Monday morning? 1030 hrs will be fine. He has achieved a very high standard while he has been here. He is just what we are looking for. Thanks Fred. See you soon."

He turned to me with a smile. "OK. 1030 hrs Monday. Very well done. I hope that the next time I see you, it will be in a Cheshire County uniform."

I thanked him for all his help, we shook hands and I went to pack my gear. As I drove away from Wrenbury Hall, I felt as though something *magic* was about to happen. I felt an incredible level of excitement. What a two-weeks it had been.

As it was to prove, those two weeks changed my entire life. I had seen a side of the ambulance service that I did not know existed until I went to Training School. The advanced training, the superb equipment and the total commitment by senior members of staff to move with the times, it was exhilarating. I wanted to be part of that! I knew that kind of training leads to experience and with that training and experience, I knew we would be able to save lives.

5. Moving to a Posh Service

I arrived at Cheadle Hulme Ambulances Station at 1015 hrs on Monday morning ready for my interview. I had taken note of how Mr. Richards at Wrenbury Hall had impressed me with his smartness and I had copied a few things from him.

I had pressed my uniform and I had spent all weekend polishing my shoes. But alas, they were only clean, not bulled. I went into the station and a well-built, happy looking man in his early forties met me. I noticed that he had the same rank markings that I had seen on Mick's uniform when I recently visited the station.

"Can I help you?" he said as I walked in.

"Good morning sir, my name is Ron Gillatt. I am here for an interview with Mr. Mitchell at 1030 hrs."

"Oh yes, we are expecting you. My name is Walter Taylor — not sir!" he said.

"Sorry, it's the white shirt and the pips," I mumbled.

"Do you want to go into that room there?" asked Walter pointing up the open stairs to the room just at the top. "That's the TV room. I will give you a shout in a few minutes. You are just a little early."

I thanked him and made my way up the stairs and sat down in the room. It was not very big but there were five armchairs in it. There was also a gents' toilet just off the room. Apart from a television and the chairs, there was nothing else in the room. I looked out the windows and to my delight, I suddenly realised that the Fire Station was adjoining the Ambulance Station. I wonder if they get on with each other. As I was looking out of the window, the fire appliance drove into in the yard and the crew started doing various drills. I watched with a degree of envy.

I had always wanted to be a full-time fireman but I was far too short. When I joined the Auxiliary Fire Service as a volunteer, it was a way of fulfilling at least some of my ambitions. I used to love drill time and turning out to fires. Occasionally we even got the chance of riding on the whole time appliances as supernumerary members of the crew. I was standing in a trance watching the firemen drilling when suddenly someone was shouting to me.

"Mr. Gillatt, could you come down please?"

I was taken into an office, which was carpeted and blue venetian blinds at the windows. There were also a number of easy chairs. There was a desk behind at which sat a very distinguished looking gentleman. He had black hair and a small moustache. It was difficult to estimate his age, but I would guess that he was in his mid-fifties. He wore a uniform and on his epaulettes were three pips. Walter had showed me into the office and he then introduced us.

"Mr. Mitchell, this is Ron Gillatt." Mr. Mitchell stood up to shake hands and as we did, I noticed that he was not much taller than I was.

"I am very pleased to meet you," he said. "Please sit down."

"Walt, would you make a brew. Coffee O.K. Ron?"

"Yes, thank you, no milk."

Walt left the office and Mr. Mitchell turned back to me. "Now then, I understand that you want to come and work here at Cheadle Hulme, is that correct?"

"Yes sir, that is right," I assured him.

"Well, Mr. Andrews has had a word with me. He tells me that you gained very high marks on your course," he started out, then he got right to the point. "That is excellent, but what I need to see is, are you going to *fit in*."

"I understand that sir, but really I would try very hard to fit in," I said.

Mr. Mitchell was stroking his moustache and looking very thoughtful. "You see, Ron, we are like a family here. In fact, most county stations operate on this basis. If you do not fit in, then the entire station will be affected," he added. "On the other hand, if you do, then we all benefit! So tell me, why do you want to come to work for Cheshire Ambulance Service?"

"Well, as you know, I work for Manchester City Ambulance Service and I have been there for a couple of years. In that time, I have gained a tremendous amount of experience mainly due to the fact that we are so busy," I explained. "But then when I went to Wrenbury Hall, I had my eyes opened. I saw equipment that I had never seen. I was taught ways of treating patients, which to you in Cheshire is routine, but they are ways that I have never been shown. I just thought how much more efficient the treatment of the patient must be in Cheshire as compared to that which I am used to. That's really why I want to come to Cheshire."

"I am pleased with your motives for wishing to move to Cheadle Hulme," he said. "And you seem to have patient care as your priority. Do you know anything about our station area?"

"No, I don't really. I know that you cover a large area."

"How do you know that, has somebody told you?"

"Yes sir. I came here a week ago yesterday to have a look around and to meet some of the staff. I was here for about two hours and I had a good talk with the Sub Officer and with the two crews who were here," I told him. "They gave me a lot of good information about the area and about the different types of incidents that you deal with."

"Well done. At least you had the initiative to come and find out for yourself."

Just then Walt reappeared with two cups of coffee. "What do you think, Walt, shall we give him a job?"

"You know my view, Mr. Mitchell. Anybody who has worked in Manchester deserves a medal!"

"Do you think you would like it here?" Walt asked me.

"Yes, I am sure I would. This would be a much more relaxed area to work in as opposed to Manchester," I said.

"You're quite right. I used to work at Belle Vue," said Walt.

"How much notice do you need to give to your service?" Mr. Mitchell enquired.

"Two weeks I think but I am not sure."

"Hmm. OK. Shall we say you will start here at 0800 hrs on 11th August?"

"Do you mean that I have got the job?" I blurted out.

"Yes. Congratulations."

They both shook hands with me and then Mr. Mitchell asked me to go upstairs to the Control Room with him. I followed him upstairs into the Control Room and I was introduced to some of the officers.

"This is Mr. Hackney. He is the Chief Control Officer and also the Assistant County Ambulance Officer. This is Ron Gillatt who will be transferring from Manchester to us in August."

Mr. Hackney stood up and to my delight, he was the same size as Mr. Mitchell and myself! He was about fifty years old and we shook hands. The phones were ringing constantly and every now and then, there would be a loud ringing noise. That was a 999 emergency call coming in.

Mr. Hackney pointed to the other staff in turn. "That's Harry Warren, that is Andy Murphy, and over there is Joe Sherwood. I hope you are a fast worker. We need fast workers here," said Mr. Hackney. "My nickname in Manchester is Fangio," I told him, figuring he knew who that was. We all did. Fangio was a world-famous motor racing driver. "They call me that because they all say that I drive that fast going to jobs!"

"You'll fit in well here then, son. See you in a few weeks."

We left the Control Room and went back to Mr. Mitchell's office.

"I hope that you will be happy here and that you find Cheshire Ambulance Service lives up to your expectations. Just remember, speed is not all that matters in the ambulance service."

As I left the office, I felt ten feet tall. I was going to get all the training and have all the facilities that the Cheshire crews took for granted. It was about nine weeks until I would start at Cheadle Hulme. Nine weeks left to work at Belle Vue Ambulance Station. To me, still being so young at the time, it seemed a lifetime away!

6. "We've Always Done It This Way"

Since it was nearly 1200 hrs by the time I left Cheadle Hulme after my interview, I did not think that it was worth going home. I would only be there for a few minutes before having to set off for work nearly straight away, so I went directly to Belle Vue. I arrived at about 1245 hrs, clocked on and went into the Mess Room. There were quite a few crews already in for lunch.

Two lads off my shift, Harry Reed and Brendan O'Donald, had been in on overtime during the morning and they had been sent in for their lunch. As I walked into the Mess Room, I was met by loud jeering from these two along with comments like, "Good afternoon, Doctor, how are you?" and "We have not seen you for two weeks. Have you been showing them what to do at the MRI (Manchester Royal Infirmary)?"

Sarcastic bastards I thought. As more and more crews came in, there was a constant light-hearted banter about the training course that I had just completed. There were also some significant and serious comments from some of the old timers. "Now that you are back from school, we will have to retrain you back to how *we* do things," they said. "Don't think that you are coming here with your *new* modern ways."

It sounded crazy. This was the summer of 1969, not the dark ages! I felt very self-conscious about their comments because I really believed that the *new ways* as they described them had potential to make a huge difference with patient care. Although patient care was good, it was good in a very limited way. Most of us really did not know any better. In other words, there was no negligence, but a person could only be as good as the training allowed them to be.

I was acutely aware that I and the few other men who had attended Wrenbury Hall for training were being pegged as *a new breed* of ambulancemen and as we all know, not everybody likes change. Change was coming in a big way and as the old saying goes, *you either go with the flow or you go!*

Bill, my regular crew mate, suddenly pushed open the Mess Room door and instantly joined in the banter that was going on as part of my *welcoming back* to duty. Bill was very interested to hear all about *"That Place"* as he called the Training School. I enthused about Wrenbury Hall and all the new procedures that I had been taught. I was keen to try some of the new techniques, but it was obvious that Bill was not. "Listen, we can't change the way that we do things," he explained. "We're are a crew and that's how we work, not as individuals."

I felt quite dejected. There I was straight back from learning the most modern techniques of patient care and I was only hearing negative comments. Bollocks, I thought. I am only here for a couple of months and then I will be working with crews who *want* to do the best that they can for their patients.

Bill and I went out for the afternoon just doing routine outpatient work and our conversation was very sporadic. I avoided any mention of *new training* but I had already decided in my own mind that when I was the attendant, I would treat the patients with the procedures that I had been taught.

The *attendant* was the crewman who actually rode in the passenger's seat and the *driver* was the other person. The *attendant's duties* were generally understood but not written down. Those duties involved the initial assessment and treatment of patients prior to moving them into the ambulance, and then providing continuing treatment where necessary in the back of the ambulance until arrival at hospital.

The *attendant's duties* also involved a detailed handover to the casualty staff at the hospital to apprise them of the patient's condition, any suspected injuries or illness, and the treatment that had been given. If it was a routine non-emergency job, the attendant was supposed to ride in the back of the ambulance with the patient. This did not always happen, and I can remember seeing ambulances arriving at casualty departments with both the driver *and* the attendant in the cab and the patient alone in the back of the ambulance. It didn't sit well with me.

This particular day with Bill, I was the *attendant* and although I was not wishing any harm to anybody, I prayed for a real juicy job just so that Bill could see how wrong he was with his obstructive attitude. I did not get my chance to show him until a few days later, but when it happened, it was my opportunity to put some of my advanced training to good use.

The late shift as it was called started at 1300 hrs and finished at 2200 hrs. I was away for the first four late shifts of this tour and returned to duty on Monday at 1300 hrs. There were five crews to a shift and on the weekday shifts, a different crew was allocated to stand-by duty each day. Stand-by meant that the allocated crew answered the 999 calls between 1300 hrs and 1400 hrs and from 1700 hrs to 2200 hrs. These shifts along with night shifts were when we saw much more action.

That week, the shifts on Monday and Tuesday were relatively quiet for Bill and me. No real serious jobs and I felt fairly disappointed in a strange way that I had not been able to "prove" myself. Then it was Wednesday and that was our last turn to do stand-by. I was the attendant and after checking our ambulance over, I called in "Foxtrot 1" to let them know we were on duty. We then retired to the Mess Room for a brew and a cigarette. Bill was in a tormenting mood and although he was generally friendly and civil, that day there was more *sarcasm*. Bill had decided that I was now acting like a *brain surgeon*, like I was so much smarter than the rest of the blokes, and it really bugged him. But those of us who had been to the Training School *really* did know better. Of course, some of the "old timers" just would not admit it.

I was sick of his attitude and the insolence that he was encouraging the other crews to display. I felt like I wanted to hit him, but I kept my cool. Instead, I found that I was talking more with the few others of us who had also attended the Training School. We had been *polarised* in such a way that we ended up offering each other support and encouragement at any times when we were not out on a shout. We agreed that we were all having to put up with the same sarcasm from the rest of the crews regardless of what shift we were on. The training had driven a wedge right through the service. It was going to be many years before attitudes would completely change.

Saved by the bell. Ring…ring…ring.

"Come on, that's for us," I said as I ran out of the Mess Room and up to the Control Room hatch. I collected the clipboard with our call sign printed on it. Clipped to it was a *pink*.

"What have we got?" asked Bill as I jumped into the passenger seat.

"A man fallen off a ladder on Scotland Hall Road, Newton Heath, time of call 1351 hrs," I reported.

"OK, off we go then," he said, setting off into the afternoon sun at a fairly steady speed. Bill was not in any hurry, but I was! As we joined a queue of traffic, I could not contain myself anymore.

"Come on, Bill, get a move on. This bloke's fallen off a ladder."

With a smug look, Bill retorted, "Taught you to be a back seat driver as well did they?"

"Look Bill, put the bell on and let's get going," I urged him.

But Bill ignored all my pleas. His attitude was typical of a few crews in our service in that era. Frequently blue lights and bells were not used. It was a kind of strange *bravado mentality* that existed with some crews. Don't ask me why, it just did.

That said, we finally arrived at the scene at 1411 hrs and as I got out of the ambulance, a huge, muscular man immediately accosted me. He was an employee at the site where we had just arrived, and he was not very happy. "Where the bloody hell have you two been? We rang up over twenty minutes ago?"

I directed him to Bill who was the driver while I was taken to see our patient. I could hear the row between Bill and the giant as I quickly followed the man ahead of me. As I approached our patient, I could see that he was moving and talking to some of his mates.

"Hello sir. I am the ambulanceman. Can you tell me what has happened to you?" I said.

"I fell off the roof, an' all these bastards are doin' is laughin'!" He was pointing to all his dust covered mates. There was still a lot of laughing and joking as I was assessing his injuries, and while doing that Bill arrived at my side.

"What have you found *Doctor*?" he said in a sarcastic way. I glared at him and asked him to get me a couple blankets from the ambulance.

"Now then sir, where does it hurt?" I asked as I turned back to the patient. He rubbed his right leg just below the knee and he also pointed out a small cut on his right hand. Before I could do or say anything, he suddenly stood up.

"I'm alright mate. I have had worse than this before," he said. I was still trying to assess the individual injuries that I *could see* and those that I *could not see* by working out the Mechanism of Injury. The Mechanism of Injury (MOI) was something that was new to everybody in the late 1960s. MOI can be described as how the injury happened and also what forces were applied to the body to produce the injury.

For example, the person who is reported as falling down the stairs may have in fact only fallen off the last step. His injuries are going to be completely different than if he had fallen from the top of the stairs and hit every step on the way down. They are both described as *falling down stairs*. How far he fell and how did he land are the key elements of the Mechanism of Injury. It is for this reason that ambulance crews always ask, "What has happened?"

In the case of our building site worker, he had fallen about eighteen feet from a roof and landed on a big pile of old roofing felt, thin pieces of old wood, empty cement bags and some cardboard. He had then apparently got up and walked over to where he was now. That was the entire MOI. He was incredibly lucky that the only thing that had been broken was his fall! No broken bones, nothing else I could see. He really was very lucky. I pointed out to him that if the pile of rubbish had not been there, he would have landed on the pavement with a completely different result. Just then, Bill returned with the blankets.

"Bloody hell! You've healed him as well," he said to me in a snarky way. "You really are something now, aren't you?"

The patient turned around and looked Bill straight in the face. "What's your bloody problem?"

Bill did not know what to say. He started to blush and mumbled, "I don't have a problem," under his breath.

"Well I think you do. There's nothing wrong with me, just a few scratches. The lad only wanted to make sure that I was alright, nothing to do with healing anything. Now sod off and leave me alone."

The patient then turned to me and said, "What's up with him?"

I did not really want to discuss it with a stranger but somehow, the circumstances just seemed wrong. I very briefly told the builder what was wrong with Bill and how I thought that he was jealous of our new training.

"Listen mate," he said to me earnestly. "You lads do a great job. Ignore the likes of him. He won't last long. Thanks for your help, but really, I am not going to hospital. I am sure I will be fine."

Since we can't force anybody to go to hospital, I asked him to sign our form declaring his refusal of hospital treatment. This done, I gathered the blankets and we left. Bill was by now in a really foul mood and although we did not argue very often, I could tell that it was about to happen.

I asked Bill to pull up so that I could complete my paperwork and after a few minutes, Bill said, "I suppose that you will be getting a secretary next." It was a fairly innocent remark but on top of all the other belittling comments that he and the other crews had made — encouraged to do so by Bill — I blew my top.

"Bill, you have become so bloody obnoxious and sarcastic since I came back from Wrenbury, you obviously do not like how I wish to work," I said. "I have been shown new ways of treating patients so that we don't cause more damage to them, better ways of immobilising fractures and many other techniques. I would like to show you, so that when we go to a job, we do it the right way, not the way we have always done it." Bill did not say anything but just stared through the windscreen.

After a few minutes, the silence was broken when Bill asked me, "Do you know how long I have been an ambulanceman?"

I looked up from filling in my pink. "No, I have no idea," I replied.

"Twenty-two years. I joined in 1947 when I came out of the army. I have seen more blood and snot than you are ever likely to see, so don't tell me how to do my job."

I tried to explain to him that I was not telling him *how* to do the job but that I thought I could show him a newer, maybe better way for the patient to be treated.

"If it was your relative, wouldn't you want the very best treatment that was available?" I asked him. But it fell on deaf ears. We snapped at each other like two Jack Russell dogs until eventually, we decided to bury the hatchet.

We agreed that when I was the attendant, Bill would try to work *my* way and when Bill was attending, we would work *his* way. I did however get him to agree to discuss all our jobs so that we both made the decision on treatment. This was a milestone!

I picked up the radio handset and called the Control.

"Foxtrot 1 to Control, over."

"Control to Foxtrot 1, go ahead, over."

"Foxtrot 1, not required at Scotland Hall Road, Newton Heath. Patient refused hospital treatment, over."

"Roger Foxtrot 1, return to station, over."

"Foxtrot 1, roger, over."

"Control, out."

Bill started the engine and drove us very sedately back to Belle Vue. We arrived back at about 1500 hrs and as we got out of the ambulance, Bill asked me about the Training School. I spent the next hour sitting in the Mess Room telling him as much as I could. He seemed genuinely interested and I thought maybe, just maybe, he really wanted to try to change his way of doing things. Just then, one of the controllers came into the Mess Room and walked through to the kitchen.

"Do you lads want a brew?" he asked.

"Ay, why not?" said Bill.

The Control Room chap was Albert Woodstock who had himself been an ambulanceman for thirty-one years before poor health had forced him to come off the road. He had very bad asthma and at least working inside kept him warm and dry.

"I hear that you've been to that new training place, Ron. What was it like?" Albert asked.

I started to describe to Albert all about the national training program and although he knew something about it, he was very interested to hear about the training that was now taking place. I told him all about Wrenbury Hall and about the course. Albert was mesmerised and kept asking questions.

"You're a lucky bugger having a mate like Ron," he said to Bill. "If only we had been able to get this type of training in my day, we would have saved a lot more lives than we did."

Bill shuffled uneasily in his chair. I told Albert that Bill was not in full agreement with the Training School and that he now thinks that I am *a doctor.* Albert then started a heated debate with Bill about how you must move with the times and Bill would be wise to take some tips from me.

Albert got up to leave the Mess Room and as he got to the door, he turned to us. "Well done, Ron. I will make sure that I send you and Bill to as many bad jobs that I can. Is that O.K with you, Ron?"

I looked at Bill's resigned expression. "It's fine by us, Albert. Thanks."

We had our tea and then went out on routine work, which involved taking people home from hospital after outpatient appointments. We collected five patients from Crumpsall Hospital (now called North Manchester General) and dropped them off one by one until we were finished at the last address in Didsbury, South Manchester.

I was about to pick up the radio when Bill said, "Let's just have five minutes."

So we sat there for a few minutes just talking about various things but strangely, nothing about training. Bill was a keen gardener and he was telling me how good his garden and his allotment were. My interest in gardens only went as far as me telling Bill about my Dad's allotment and how he had let me have "my own little garden" when I was a young boy.

We were chatting away as though there had never been any acrimony between us. In fact, it was just like it had been before I had gone to school. The peace was suddenly shattered by the radio bursting to life.

The control was trying to find an ambulance crew to attend an emergency call in a district a couple of miles away from where we were. "Any crew for a Motorcyclist RTA (Road Traffic Accident) in Rusholme, over." I looked at Bill and went to pick up the radio to answer the request.

"Leave it, they will find somebody else, we were just having a nice chat," suggested Bill.

"Bill, there is nobody else. That's why Albert is shouting for a crew." I picked up the radio and spoke into the microphone.

"Foxtrot 1 to Control, over.

"Go ahead, Foxtrot 1, over.

"Foxtrot 1, clear in Didsbury if that is any help for the RTA, over."

"Many thanks Foxtrot 1, please attend a Motorcyclist RTA at the junction of Hathersage Road and Wilmslow Road, Rusholme. Time 1812 hrs, over."

"Foxtrot 1, roger, over."

"Roger Foxtrot 1, Control out."

Bill started the engine and off we went. He had switched on the little blue light, which was about the size of a coffee mug, and he was using the bell! This was really a change for Bill from his previous way of thinking. The bell was useless of course since most people could not hear it. It was quite often more dangerous to use the bell than to not use it. That was because ringing it gave the driver a false sense of security: we could just about hear the bell in the cab and as such, we assumed that everybody else around us could hear it.

As we approached the RTA, I could see a very large crowd of people opposite the actual junction of Hathersage Road, which formed a "T" junction with Wilmslow Road. Hathersage Road was a fairly busy road and so was Wilmslow Road. Opposite Hathersage Road was a park, which was surrounded by iron railings. Bill pulled up and we both got out.

Being the attendant, I made my way through the crowd as best as I could. Being short really does have a lot of problems so I was forced to push and shove my way through. I finally got through to where I saw the patient. He appeared to be very seriously injured and there was a lot of blood on the sidewalk. The motorcycle was on its side with quite a lot of petrol dripping out of the tank.

It appeared that the motorcyclist had been riding down Hathersage Road towards the "T" junction with Wilmslow Road. He had apparently failed to stop at the junction, gone straight across the road, mounted the pavement and crashed into the railings. The moment that the bike hit the kerb, the rider was thrown off and catapulted into the iron railings.

I knelt down and noticed that he was unresponsive.

"Hello, can you hear me?" I shouted in his ear. There was no response.

I gave him a very gentle shake and at the same time I shouted again, "Can you hear me?" There was still no response.

I was about to start examining him when Bill appeared through the crowd. He turned to the huge throng and shouted in a booming voice, "Everybody move back. Give us some space to work!" He then turned quickly to me. "O.K. Ron, what do you need?"

"I don't know, Bill, I was just about to check him over."

"Is he with us?" Bill asked.

"No, he's well out. Find his helmet, we need to look at it."

Bill picked it up and looked at me with an enquiring look on his face. "I am looking at his helmet but what am I looking for?" asked Bill.

"Look at the impact mark and the scrape marks. His head hit something very hard. No wonder he is unconscious." Bill grunted in agreement.

I examined the patient further and discovered that he had what felt like unusual lumps on each thigh. I had also found that the left side of his chest felt spongy.

"Bill, we need to open his jacket and we need to have a better look at the tops of his legs. I think that both his femurs have open fractures. I also think that he has severe damage to his chest on the left side."

Bill listened to my diagnosis and then said, "Good enough for me mate, what do you need?"

"Will you check him and tell me what you think?"

In an instant, Bill was doing an examination. After a couple of minutes, he announced his agreement with my opinion.

"Help me open his trousers, Bill, so that we can see his thighs."

With a little difficulty, we managed to get to the top of his trousers and undo them. In the meantime, the patient had started to make some low moaning sounds, so we were pleased that at least he was making some noise! We peered down at his thighs and we were astounded to see that both femurs were clearly broken and the ends were protruding through the skin for several inches!

We carefully placed dressings over the ends of the bones and the wounds. The spongy feeling in his chest had also given us cause for concern and when we finally opened his jacket, the damage was revealed. About two pounds of tomatoes in a paper bag were now purée! He had been carrying them inside his jacket and of course, they had become squashed!

Bill went to the ambulance for the stretcher and some triangular bandages with which we could tie the patient's legs together. This would help to stop his legs moving when we lifted him onto the stretcher. With help from bystanders, Bill carried the stretcher and placed it next to the patient.

I worked fairly quickly with Bill's help tying the legs together. We were still constantly checking to see if the patient had started to respond, but he was still just making the moaning noises. Finally, we were ready to move him. Bill organised some hefty looking bystanders to help. We had seven of us in total. I was about to say to them all what we were going to do when Bill piped up with a voice of authority. "Right now, listen to what my mate says and do exactly as he tells you!"

"Thanks Bill. OK, we all lift at the same time straight onto the stretcher. I will hold his head and we will lift on three." "One, two, three lift."

It went very smoothly and in no time, the helpers were asking if we needed anything else doing. "Could you help us to carry him into the ambulance, please?" said Bill.

As the doors of the ambulance closed, I was setting up the oxygen mask and adjusting the flow rate. The patient was still making some groaning noises which showed an improvement from his initial unresponsive state.

Bill started the engine. "Tell me when you are ready to go, Ron."

The hospital was only about half a mile away so the journey was short. "Whenever you are ready Bill, just a nice steady run please."

In no time at all we arrived at Manchester Royal Infirmary Casualty Department, which was their emergency department. A number of other ambulance crews were standing around talking as we arrived. Bill stopped the ambulance and came around to open the rear doors.

"Oh, you have the Brain Surgeon with you today, Bill! Saved many lives on this shift?"

Bill just gave them a withering look as we unloaded our casualty. Once inside the casualty department, a couple of nurses and a doctor turned to Bill and asked him for details of the accident and our suspicion of injuries.

"You need to ask my mate, Ron. He did all the examining and I think he knows."

So I started to give a reasonably detailed handover and I asked Bill to bring in the motorcyclists helmet from the ambulance. As the doctor supervised the undressing of the casualty, I started to show him the helmet and the damage to it. I thought that it was significant and so did the doctor.

"Teaching you lads about Mechanism of Injury (MOI) now are they?" Bill looked slightly puzzled but nodded. I told the doctor that I had recently been on the new advanced training course and that was where I gained some knowledge of MOI. The doctor was very impressed and made the point that not enough ambulance crews understand the importance of that concept.

After we had both been given a pat on the back from the doctor, we washed down the stretcher and ourselves and tidied the back of the ambulance as we prepared for our next call. Bill asked me if we could discuss the motorcycle accident in detail. I told Bill that I was very happy to chat about it. Was this going to be another argument I thought or was this where Bill might start to change his attitude?

As we left the casualty department, Bill drove into the very large hospital parking area and picked a parking spot. After turning off the engine, Bill asked again about the marks on the motorcyclists helmet.

"What were you looking for? We have never done that before," he asked.

So I started to explain how there are visual pieces of information which are not necessarily injuries, that can give good clues to potential injuries.

There may be damaged clothing, damaged shoes or boots and of course, the scrape marks on a motorcycle helmet or on a construction hard hat.

"I know that we have never done this before, Bill, but it is something that is now being introduced as part of the National Training Program for the whole country," I said. "The main reason for doing those quick checks is to have an idea where there might be *hidden* injuries."

Bill seemed to think that it would not "catch on" as he put it, but I pointed out that this was the way Ambulance Service training was progressively changing and that everybody who took that new training would be working this way.

The remainder of the tour of duty was relatively quiet with just a number of minor emergency calls made up of drunks, seizure patients, falls and a variety of others. We finished our lates at 2200 on Monday. Our next shift together was going to be *nights* starting Thursday evening at 2200 hrs. I was really looking forward to this tour because when we did nights, we could run into anything and everything! And that night, I had no idea how *right* I would be.

7. Nights and Days

Thursday came around very quickly and I arrived at the station at 2130 hrs — half an hour before the start of the shift. All the late shift crews were out on calls so after I put my supper into my locker, I went to get our ambulance ready for work. I checked the engine oil level, the coolant, the tyres and then I did a walk around the outside looking for any dents, scratches or damage that might have been done while we were off duty.

Everything was OK so I checked inside the back of the ambulance. Stretcher, six blankets, pillow, first aid box, and oxygen cylinder contents. Yes, correct. With that complete, I went to the Mess Room and made tea and coffee for all the five crews who were about to come on duty. By this time, it was 2155 hrs. Men started to arrive and general good-hearted banter started. Bill arrived and looked reasonably happy. As I had made the brews, I offered it around and everybody had a mug full of tea or coffee.

On night shift, crews went out on calls in a set order. Since there were five crews to a shift, the crews were numbered one to five depending on which line number you were on the roster. Bill and I were on line five, so we were last out. Suddenly, the bells rang three times and the first crew was gone! That was 2204 hrs.

Bill said that we better check the ambulance, but I told him I had already done that and that really pleased him. Maybe we will have a happy tour on nights. I was open to wait and see!

We sat in the Mess Room chatting about what we had done on our days off and Bill told me about his garden and about some plants he had planted. I know very little about gardening but I do know how to service and repair cars. I told him that I had done a couple of car jobs for friends and earned a little bit of money doing it. Suddenly three more rings rang out, and another crew was gone. It was 2225 hrs.

Within a minute, another three bells and off went the third crew. It was starting to get busy.

At 2241 hrs, the bells went again and then again. *Was that for two crews?* We quickly went up to the Control Room hatch and Albert was shouting to both crews to attend a serious call. "House Fire — Persons Reported." *Persons Reported* is a Fire Brigade term adopted by the ambulance service and it indicates that people are reported trapped. Bill and I were out of the station first with the second crew on this call about a hundred yards behind us. The call was to Massey Street in the district of Moss Side which was about five miles away.

Moss Side in the late 1960s was a rundown district designated for demolition. It had been a very highly desirable area in which to live forty or fifty years before that but now it was slowly being demolished. In the future, there would be a more modern and newer housing development in place of the old run down area we used to visit.

That night, Bill was driving well and traffic was light, so we were soon travelling through Moss Side towards Massey Street. As we rounded a slight bend on Moss Lane East, we could see a lot of smoke above the rooftops on our left. There were also a number of fire appliances parked haphazardly in the roadway.

"This looks like a bad one," I said to Bill as he was coming to a stop. It was now 2252 hrs.

"Let's hope everybody is out safely," Bill replied.

The house was an old Victorian house of three floors, quite typical of the property in that area. As we quickly made our way on foot along the street to the actual house, we could see smoke billowing out of the front top floor windows and little sparks breaking through the roof.

The street was lined on both sides with parked cars and the fire engines were down the centre of the street, hoses snaking from hydrants to the fire engines and from the fire engines to various firemen who were inside the house and also in the street.

As we got closer to the house, we got our first view of the catastrophe. We were looking at the almost burned out shell of the ground floor of the house and the second floor the same, although the top floor and most of the roof were intact. While we searched for a fire officer to report to, we were suddenly aware that there was a loud shout from somewhere in the pandemonium: "You two, stay back, stay well back!"

"We are the Ambulance Service. Is everybody out OK?" Bill called out.

The shout to *stay back* had come from a Leading Fireman who was just coming out of what was left of the front door of the house.

"Just stay back, lads, this is a bloody bad one," he said. "Nobody is out yet. We are trying to get up the stairs to the top floor, but most of the stairs are burned away."

Ladders had already been raised to some of the upper windows and a few more ladders were being taken into the house so that the firemen could try to get up to the different floors from the inside. With no casualties out of the house, which was at that moment just a charred and smoking mess, this was probably a fatal fire.

There was a large number of firemen who had been battling this fire and some were carrying equipment into the house, including a ceiling hook which is a long wooden pole with a large hook fixed at a right angle at the top. It's usually used for pulling down what remained of the ceiling in order to reveal any area still smouldering.

Then a Fire Brigade officer came past us and told us again to wait, nobody was out yet. Some firemen were struggling to pitch a ladder to a room where there was smoke pouring out of a window on the top floor. Another fireman ran over to help them and after a few moments, a fireman ran up the ladder with a hose over his shoulder. As soon as the first fireman was about half-way up the ladder, a second fireman ran up the ladder after him.

We could see that as soon as the first fireman reached the top of the ladder, he disappeared into the dense smoke. The second fireman was supporting the heavy hose and shouting to the fireman who had gone into the room. Large volumes of smoke and steam told us that the assault on the fire in that room had started!

The noise and smell was incredible, not just from the fire and smoke but from the pumps on the fire engines screaming, people shouting and of course civilians distraught and crying uncontrollably. The smoke was so thick and acrid that it was difficult to see through it at times. It was sheer mayhem! Our second ambulance crew had joined us by this time and asked us about casualties. When we told them what the fire officer had told us, we all started to realise that this was indeed a bad one.

We were at the scene for over an hour and eventually the fire officer came to talk to us.

"Hi Ron, I thought it was you. What are you doing here?" He looked puzzled as he looked at my uniform. "So are you with the Ambulance Service now?"

It was Station Officer Singleton speaking and he has been in charge of a fire station where I worked as a volunteer fireman.

"Yes sir, this looks a bad one?"

"We have two adults which we do not know if they are male or female because they are so badly burned and we have three children of various sizes also burned beyond recognition."

"Bloody hell, five people in all?" I gasped.

"Yes, this was a death trap, paraffin heaters on every floor and cans of extra paraffin stored in the rooms where the heaters were. It went up like a torch. We had no chance of getting in initially."

That area was occupied mostly by people from the Caribbean islands and Jamaica in particular. Even in warmer weather there was a tendency to have paraffin heaters in most rooms, and this was the situation tonight. Our other crew had left the scene once it became obvious that it was a fatal fire. Nobody had any idea of the scale of the tragedy but the fact that no casualties were going to be coming out of the fire, that fact became a foregone conclusion.

Station Officer Singleton came over to tell us that the bodies would not be removed for several hours and the Fire Brigade no longer needed us at the scene. Bill suggested that since this would be a coroner's job, we should find the police officer in charge and ask if we could be released.

We were given clearance to leave by the police in charge, Chief Inspector Jordan, and made our way carefully over hoses and other fire brigade equipment back to our ambulance. We smelled like a pair of smoked kippers after being in all that smoke! We sat there for a few minutes thinking about the fire and the number of fatalities.

I called the Control.

"Foxtrot 1 to base, over."

"Foxtrot 1, over"

"Foxtrot 1, now clear at Massey Street, Moss Side. Fatal House Fire, five DOAs (Dead on Arrival). We have been released by Chief Inspector Jordan, Police Officer in charge at the fire, over."

There was silence for about half a minute and then, "Foxtrot 1, did you say five DOAs?"

"Foxtrot 1, roger, five, over."

"Roger Foxtrot 1, I have an emergency call for you on Oxford Road near to the BBC Studios in the City, a drunk with a cut arm, time 0010 hrs, over."

"Foxtrot 1, roger, over."

Bill drove at a reasonable pace to our next call on Oxford Road, arriving at 0017 hrs. We were met by a number of members of the public who were mostly the worse for the drink. We found our casualty and as we tried to examine his injury, eight or nine drunken individuals all started to tell us how to do our job! They were trying to drag the injured man to the back of the ambulance. We were in no mood to argue with them especially coming from the fatal fire. But they all thought that they knew better than us what to do with the injured man!

Bill politely told them all to move away and allow us to see the man's injury. Just then, a policeman arrived and then two more. As if by magic, the crowd dispersed and we final had a look at the injury. It was a scratch! Like a cat might do if it caught you with its claws. This did not even need a dressing but since it was a 999 call, we had to take the drunken lout to the hospital. The MRI was only a mile away and we were there in just a few minutes. We handed over our cut-arm casualty and finally we hoped that we were going back to the station for a meal.

"Foxtrot 1 to base, over."

"Foxtrot 1 over."

"Foxtrot 1 clear at MRI, over"

"Foxtrot 1 return to station. over"

"Foxtrot 1 roger, over"

"Foxtrot 1, base out."

We arrived back on station at 0045 hrs, hoping for a meal break. All the other crews were back in so we were 5th out again. There was a good chance of a sit down and a meal.

The rest of the night was relatively quiet until 0650 hrs.

We were next out and as I collected the pink ticket, the information just read "Male heart attack," in the district of Levenshulme.

Levenshulme was about three miles from the station. Bill set off driving into the early morning traffic and we were soon approaching the address. A lady who looked distraught was standing in the street waving us down. As we stopped, I jumped out and I was met with the lady just screaming! I tried to get information from her but it was no use, she was panic stricken and incoherent.

Bill joined me and between us we gained fragments of information. It seemed that she had called us because her husband who was upstairs in bed had severe chest pains. I went into the house and up the stairs where I saw a man of about fifty years old and of quite slim build. He was ashen, grey in appearance and sweating profusely. He told me that he had been woken up with the pains in the centre of his chest around 0330 but now they were getting worse. Bill had followed me into the bedroom and asked me what did I think and what did I need.

I told Bill in a low voice that I was sure that this was an "MI" (Myocardial Infarction — medical terminology for a heart attack). Bill nodded in agreement and went off for some blankets and a fold up carry chair which we used to carry people downstairs and into the ambulance. We were fortunate to have a carry chair on this ambulance as only a few had recently been issued.

I started to examine the patient and to get some prior history from him. It transpired that the patient had a minor heart attack two years ago and was taking medication for the condition. Just as I was finishing my checks, his wife appeared in the bedroom, still crying and actually making the situation worse. Then Bill arrived with the chair and blankets and we ushered the lady out of the room and back down the stairs.

We wrapped the patient tightly in the blankets so that he could not *grab out* as we carried him downstairs. People being carried downstairs on a carry chair are frequently very nervous. I knew this because we had practiced the use of the carry chair at Training School and it is a strange feeling. Often the patient will grab at the banister rail because they think that the crew is about to drop them. A good crew can do a very stable rapid decent of a flight of stairs perfectly steadily.

As we carried the patient into the ambulance, he suddenly became unresponsive. We quickly lifted him onto the stretcher and as Bill was closing the back doors, the patient's wife came running out of the house and joined us in the back of the ambulance.

I had already started to administer oxygen and had put the patient into the best position for his condition. In those days, different casualty departments wanted cardiac related patients in different positions. Some hospitals insisted on the patient being in a sitting-up position, some wanted the person lying flat and some did not have an opinion one way or the other. I knew it was important to remember how each hospital wanted things done.

His wife kept standing up and I told her to sit down as we cannot move until she was sitting. There were no seat belts in those days. She finally sat down and off we went to hospital. The patient was on oxygen but still unresponsive. His colour was slightly better, but he was clearly in a very bad way.

In those days in Manchester, we did not have any equipment to do anymore for the patient. I had been trained in airway management techniques at the Training School using disposable Oropharyngeal Airways (OPAs) but we did not have that equipment. OPAs are a curved, short plastic tube that is inserted into the mouth and throat of an unresponsive patient in order to prevent the airway from being blocked by the tongue. I wondered how the Cheshire crews would have dealt with this incident with all the new and most modern equipment at the ready. It would not be long now before I would find out, but that night, I was using what we had on hand and doing my best.

We arrived at the hospital after a very smooth ride and just as Bill opened the back doors, he asked how things were. "He's still with us, Bill, but still unresponsive."

Bill gave me an odd look as we unloaded the patient and took him into the casualty department. I did the handover and finished my paperwork then back to the ambulance to tidy up ready for the next job. When we were tidying up, Bill asked, "What is this *unresponsive?* We always say *unconscious.*"

"Well, *unconscious* means different things to different people so the word *unresponsive* is used instead," I explained. "When checking a patient, I check for alertness, response to my voice, or response to pain. If the patient does not respond to those three assessments then they are *unresponsive*. It is part of the new training terminology."

Bill just grunted and mumbled something unintelligible under his breath.

"Foxtrot 1 to base, over.

"Base to Foxtrot 1."

"Foxtrot 1, clear MRI, over."

"Foxtrot 1, return to base, over."

"Foxtrot 1, roger."

"Base out."

We arrived back on station at 0755 hrs, just in time to finish our shift at 0800. That was a night that I will never forget.

I was back to work on Friday, and it was usually a busy shift with a wide variety of calls and particularly calls involving alcohol. When the pubs closed, that was when the calls increased in number. Bill had taken some leave and so I was crewed up with a Shift Leader on his ambulance. His name was Tom Ferguson and although I knew him, I had not worked with him before.

He was fairly enthusiastic about the extended training and asked me to be the *attendant* and he would drive. That suited me. Tom also said that he would follow whatever I suggested for the treatment of our patients. His attitude was a change for me since it was quite a different attitude compared to my regular mate I thought.

After checking our ambulance, call sign Echo 2, we went for a cup of coffee. Tom was a smoker and he rolled his own cigarettes. I found it fascinating to watch him complete the task of making a cigarette just using one hand.

We were second out that night and we were expecting the bells to start at any minute. Time passed and the first crew did not get turned out until 2255 hrs. That was very rare on a Friday night to have that first call not come in until around that time. Usually all five crews would be out on calls by then.

We waited and waited and at 2314 hrs, ring, ring, ring.

"That's us, Ron. You get the job and I'll start her up."

In a flash I had collected the emergency call pink and I had jumped into the passenger seat.

"What have we got, Ron?" asked Tom.

"A Fall Downstairs, at 46 East Road, Longsight," I told him. East Road was about two and a half miles away and although there was still some traffic on the roads, it was a fairly easy drive. We arrived at the house and found that the front door was open and a number of people were in the hallway obscuring our view of the patient who was lying at the bottom of the stairs.

Within a few moments, we realised that most of the people appeared to have consumed alcohol in varying quantities. They were all talking at the same time in loud voices. We tried to announce our arrival, but nobody was listening. They were actually trying to get the casualty to stand up. Tom had joined me and as if we had rehearsed it, we both shouted at the same time in our very loud voices: "Quiet please!"

There was instant silence and we asked the group of maybe eight or nine people if anybody actually saw what had happened. Three people claimed to know what transpired, so while Tom gathered information about the incident from them, I talked to the patient and checked him for injuries.

When large quantities of drink have been consumed, the patient may not feel all their injuries so it was always essential to do a full examination. I worked methodically and slowly checking him from head to foot. The only injuries I could find appeared to be a small lump on his head and some grazes and small cuts on his bare arms and hands.

It would seem that the patient had fallen from about the third step up on the stairs and not all the way down as we might have thought. Tom asked me what did I think.

"Well, he has a bump on head so we should take him to the MRI," I said.

"That's good enough for me, Ron.

"Let's see if he can get up, Tom."

We explained to the patient that we were going to take him to hospital to have him checked over and he seemed happy about that. Between us, we got him to his feet and since he was fairly unsteady, probably due to the drink, we walked with him between us out of the house and into the ambulance.

I sat down next to the patient who now thought he might want to be sick. We used to scrounge papier-mâché vomit bowls from the different hospitals and we always had some handy for just this occasion. I handed a vomit bowl to the patient as Tom closed the back doors and off we went to hospital. It was only about a ten-minute drive but in that time the patient had easily filled two vomit bowls with mostly beer.

Tom opened the back doors and I helped our patient out of the ambulance and into a wheelchair that was nearby. Tom pushed him into the department and I got rid of the vomit bowls. After a quick handover it was time for a wash and we also looked around to scrounge some replacement bowls.

When we got back into the ambulance, Tom started to ask about the extended training course that I had attended and also, how was Bill doing with the new procedures. I did not really want to discuss Bill but I outlined the new training. Tom seemed impressed and said that he was looking forward to seeing me *doing more of that stuff*, as he put it.

"Echo 2 to base over."

"Base, Echo 2."

"Echo 2, clear at MRI, over."

"Roger, Echo 2, return to base, 0005 over."

"Roger."

"Base out."

"You can work with me again anytime, Ron. I have never known it to be so quiet on a Friday night," he said.

"Well, it's only just gone midnight. Eight hours to go!" I said.

We arrived back on station at around 0020 hours and we were last out. It was a very quiet night and although a few crews went out on emergency calls, we were not called again until 0310 hrs.

Ring, ring, ring. This time it was to a Road Traffic Accident (RTA) on Wilmslow Road in the district of Rusholme which was about four miles away. As Tom was driving to the scene, our radio suddenly burst into life. I picked up the handset and answered the call.

"Base, Echo 2, over."

"Echo 2 to base, over."

"Echo 2, further information on the RTA that you are attending, the car is folded around a lamppost and the driver is trapped. Fire Brigade on route, over."

"Echo 2, roger, over."

"Base out."

"Sounds interesting," I commented to Tom.

"Well, you're the man for the job, Ron. Maybe you can use some of your new skills," said Tom.

"I certainly hope not," I said. "I don't want to wish somebody badly injured just so I can put some of the new procedures into practice."

As we approached the scene, it became obvious that the car had hit the kerb edge which had rolled it onto its side. It had then slid along the road on its side and finally crashed into a steel lamppost with the roof first, hitting right in the centre of the roof. The car had then virtually folded in half around the lamppost.

"What a bloody mess," said Tom.

As we got out of the ambulance, I went to look for the driver and since I could only look into the car through the opening where the rear window used to be and it was the same situation at the front of the car, it was really difficult to see anything.

After a few moments, I spotted the driver in a heap in the front area of the car on what would be the inside of the driver's door and he was not moving. I called to Tom to bring some blankets and between us, we were able to cover him up. I scrambled into the car and started to assess the patient. Because of the damage to the car, there was not much room to move. Good job I am small I thought!

The fire brigade arrived quickly, and Tom told them what the situation was. I stayed inside the car with the patient while Tom spoke to the Fire Officer about how we were going to get the patient out. In those days, the fire brigade had an air powered Cengar Saw, which was like a hack saw but it was powered off of a breathing apparatus air cylinder or in some cases, a small compressor. They also had a hydraulic ram type tool called a "Porta Power" which was used for spreading. As you can imagine, releasing trapped patients was a relatively slow job in those days.

"They are going to do some cutting. How is he doing?" asked Tom.

"Well, he's still unresponsive, but I have not found any bleeding. I think it is a head injury," I reported. "I'm also worried about his airway. It seems partly obstructed, probably by his tongue." The airway basically consists of the mouth, nose, throat, and windpipe. It can become blocked anywhere along its length and death will result very quickly if the airway is fully blocked.

"What do you mean *unresponsive*?" he said.

"I'll explain later, Tom," I told him, returning my focus to the patient. In my mind, I thought, here we go again. Maybe for the next few weeks, I should use the old fashioned word: *unconscious*.

"What's this airway problem?" asked Tom. "We don't usually deal with the airway. That's the doctor's job, not ours, right?"

I ignored the comment and I tried to look into the patients' mouth but without a torch (flashlight) it was difficult. I shouted to Tom to see if the fire crew had a spare torch and luckily, they did. I could now do a proper airway check and fortunately, there was no blockage. But I did find out that the position of his head was the reason for his difficulty in breathing.

I stayed with the patient for over a half an hour securing his head in case of a spinal injury until he could been freed. Before we moved him, I immobilized his neck by making a *cervical collar* out of a tightly rolled blanket in order to protect his neck. It was then a case of removing him carefully from the car and onto the stretcher which Tom had prepared ready to receive the patient. We managed the delicate move and with the patient on the stretcher, a few firemen helped carry him into the ambulance.

The injured man was still very quiet, but his breathing had improved once I put him on oxygen. Tom closed the doors and off we went, the half mile to the MRI. I did a hand over to the nurses and the doctor as Tom hovered in the background. I told the staff that I thought this was a head injury and that was why I had made the collar from a blanket.

"I've never seen that done before. Is it a new procedure?" asked the doctor.

Before I could answer, Tom explained the Advanced Training course that a few of the ambulance staff have been on.

"This is really impressive stuff," said the doctor. "Well done to both of you."

Tom was smiling as we loaded the stretcher back into the ambulance.

"You scored a hit with that doctor," said Tom.

"*We* did," I reminded Tom. "He told you well done as well."

"What is this bloody *unresponsive*?" blurted out Tom, barely able to contain his curiosity any longer. I gave him the explanation I had learned and he seemed happy to tuck that information away for future reference.

The rest of the week was a mixture of minor emergency calls and alcohol related calls.

By this time, it was only a few more weeks until I would start working for Cheshire County Ambulance Service and as I had some leave to take anyway, I decided to give my notice in to Manchester City Ambulance Service and take a week off on leave right away.

When we were back on day shift, as I walked into the station, I noticed Bill's car was parked in his usual parking spot. Bill always parked in the same place every shift, a creature of habit. Bill had returned to duty after his leave and he seemed quite jovial and happy to be back. I thought, this was a good time to tell Bill about my imminent transfer to the Cheshire Ambulance Service.

As I told Bill about my appointment with Cheshire, he did not really comment except to ask me why I had not told him before now. He just looked resigned to having a new permeant crew mate and just remarked, "Well, at least I can get back to working my way and not all your doctoring methods!"

"Those kind of comments are *why* I am transferring, Bill," I said bluntly.

Bill became suddenly became very irate.

"Well, do you think things are any better in Cheshire than they are here? Cheshire are known for their over the top treatment instead of getting the patient moved to the hospital," he argued. "They spend all their time *playing at doctors.*"

"I don't want to have this discussion, Bill," I concluded. "I am leaving Manchester on August 10th and I start at Cheshire on August 11th and it is what I want to do."

I went to see the boss in order to give him my notice of intention to leave on August 10th. I explained my reasons and he said that he was sorry to see me go but he fully understood and wished me well. I told Bill that I had put in my notice, but he did not say anything.

He was very quiet for the remainder of the day and since we were just doing out-patient transport on those particular shifts, it suited me perfectly. We both maintained a civil attitude to each other and at the end of the day, we both had a coffee and a polite, but guarded, chat before going home.

Finally, I was going into my last week at Manchester and I was itching to start at my new service. That last week at work, we were on lates and we started at 1300 hrs. I arrived for work at 1240 hrs wondering what sort of mood Bill would be in. I thought about all the sarcasm that I had been subjected to since Training School and I decided that what they had done to me and the other blokes was really like bullying and abuse.

I checked the ambulance and went into the Mess Room where there were a few crews in having their lunch. One or two asked if it was true that I was leaving and I told them I was going to Cheshire County.

"Oh, going working in the snobby area, are you?" commented Paul Dixon with whom I had spent my very first day on operations. I remember the maggot-ridden green man. I never could forget that job.

"I don't know the area where I will be working," I told him. "The station is in a district called Cheadle Hulme"

"Cheadle Hulme is the area where all the bloody snobs live," he sputtered. "More Rolls Royces than anywhere else!"

"Those snobs all think that they are better than everybody else," said Ron Green.

Just then Bill walked into the Mess Room with a face like thunder.

Oh hell, I thought. This is going to be a tense shift.

"Hi everybody," said Bill in a very friendly way.

"Hi Bill," I replied but my reply was met by a glaring expression.

After a few moments, I asked Bill to go outside with me which he reluctantly did. Almost immediately a massive row started with me telling Bill what I thought of his bullying behaviour and his sarcastic comments that had gone on for several months. He told me that I now thought that I was better than he was. I tried to explain that I was *better trained* than he was, but he just walked away and back into the Mess Room.

Shortly after our disagreement, we were sent out on out-patient work which continued until about 1625 hrs. When we dropped our last patient off, the radio suddenly barked into life: "Base to any crew for a scalding incident in Wythenshawe, over." Wythenshawe is a huge sprawling area in the south of Manchester. We were about five or six miles away, so we did not answer.

"Base to any crew for a baby scalded in Wythenshawe — urgently, over."

Silence from Bill. I finally said, "We should answer that call, Bill, nobody else is."

"We're too far away, leave it," he said.

"No, I am answering it, Bill."

"Foxtrot 1, base, over."

"Base to Foxtrot 1, over."

"Foxtrot 1, we are clear in Fallowfield if we are any use for the scalding call, over."

"Foxtrot 1, thank you. Please attend at Poundswick Lane, Wythenshawe, a ten-month-old baby scalded, time is 1625 hrs. I will cancel you if I get anybody nearer. Base out."

I think Bill's irritability at me calling Control regarding the emergency had resulted in a positive effect on him after all because he drove like a man possessed. We flew through the streets and at 1647 hrs, we arrived at the scene.

I jumped out and went into the house through the open door. I could hear lots of shouting and a baby screaming like I had never heard one scream before. I was shouting to try and attract the attention of somebody in the house but their level of panic and screaming drowned out my attempts to attract attention.

I followed the noise and ended up in a bedroom upstairs and for the first time saw the source of the screaming. The baby was lying on a bed with the distraught mother uncontrollably sobbing. I examined the baby and to my horror nearly all the skin on the baby's back was hanging down like ribbons! There were also areas on the front of the baby's legs where the skin had shrivelled up and peeled off.

In those days, we did not have anything with which to treat burns so I asked the mother for a couple of clean pillowcases that we could use to wrap the baby in. In a flash, she produced the items and with great difficulty I was able to wrap the worst areas with the cotton pillowcases. Remember, we did not have gloves in those days, so all our work was done "bare-handed." Bill asked me if there was anything he could do, and I asked him to steady me as I carried the screaming baby down the stairs and into the ambulance.

As Bill closed the backdoors, I asked him to notify the casualty department at Wythenshawe Hospital of our impending arrival and the condition of our baby. It transpired that the mother had been running a bath for the baby but forgot to check the temperature. As she lowered the baby into the bath, she suddenly felt how hot it was but struggled to lift the instantly screaming baby out of the bath for a second or two. The damage had been done and could have been fatal.

Bill did a very fast drive and as we arrived at the casualty department, a team of nurses and doctors were waiting for us. The casualty department was very old as was most of this part of the hospital. But the team sprang into action and I did my handover immediately. As I watched them work, a senior nurse told me that this type severe of injury was rare and usually when that amount of area of the body was affected, the patient might not survive.

I watched as they cut all the loose skin off and set up IVs for fluids and drugs. I had never seen scalds that severe on a baby before and the image of the injury became imprinted in my mind and it still is. I can still hear the screams and see the scalds even now as I write this, 50 years later.

Bill was very quiet as we tidied up the back of the ambulance and as I was getting out he suddenly said, "I'm glad you took that call. I am very sorry that I told you to leave it and not answer the radio."

I just looked at Bill. I did not know what to say. Bill had never apologized for anything that had happened previously, especially not for the obstructive or downright aggressive things he said and did towards me.

I think that he was shaken up a bit by the whole thing. I know I was too. This job had hit me very hard, both from frustration at no equipment for burns, but this was the first severe scalds to a baby that I had dealt with. I was inwardly quite distressed that day and I thanked Bill for his comments and understanding. I asked Bill why he had made his apologetic comments. He did not answer but just smiled.

"I'll tell you one day," said Bill.

"Well, you better hurry up, Bill. I leave in a couple of weeks!" I reminded him.

"Foxtrot 1, base."

"Base, Foxtrot 1, over."

"Foxtrot 1, clear at Wythenshawe."

"Roger Foxtrot 1, return to station, over."

"Foxtrot 1, roger."

"Base out."

Bill and I were in a sombre mood as we set off to drive the forty-five minutes back to station. There was not much conversation between us but what there was seemed quite normal. We arrived back on station, washed and tidied the ambulance and then just as we were about to go home, Bill suddenly asked me if I had a few minutes to chat. I thought, what is this going to be about?

"Yes, of course, what is the problem Bill?" He had a strange look on his face which I had not seen before.

"You don't have kids, do you Ron?" he said.

"No Bill, I am not married. You?"

"I had three, two boys and a girl, one died."

"Bloody hell, Bill, sorry to hear that." I was not sure what else to say.

"My girl died when she was five. She was burned to death. Her dress caught fire and the flames engulfed her. She died three days later." By this time, Bill was sobbing his heart out and I was close to it. I tried to comfort Bill but there was nothing that I could say that would help.

"That was eight years ago," said Bill through his sobs. "I'm OK now but some jobs just bring it all back, and that scalding job. That was why I did not want you to answer the radio. I knew it would trigger it all off again, but I am glad that you did answer the radio. We might have possibly saved a life."

I was still trying to comfort Bill and he was settling down a little.

"Thanks for listening, Ron. I cannot talk to anybody else about this, only my workmates. Only they understand what we go through day after day and what triggers off things like our baby scalded," Bill explained. "Don't bottle things up, Ron. Talk to the friends that you have who are on the job.

This isn't the kind of talk to have with people outside, not somebody who just wants to hear about *what you do.*"

I went home seriously thinking about Bill's advice and I still think about it now, but for a different reason.

Before I knew it, it was my last day of working for Manchester Ambulance Service. I arrived for duty at 1230 on Sunday, August 10th. It felt very strange being so excited about starting work for a different Ambulance Service. Bill arrived shortly after me and we had a nice chat, checked the ambulance and then settled down in the Mess Room. Our conversation was jolly with lots of banter and I wondered why this had not happened before. Maybe Bill was glad he was *getting rid* of me at the end of the shift?

Sunday shifts were unpredictable but generally they were not too busy. On this day we did not go out until 1540 hrs and that was only to take somebody home after treatment in the casualty department.

Our next job was at 2050 hrs, ring, ring, ring. I collected the pink ticket and it was to an RTA in Clayton, a district about a ten-minute drive from the station. I was driving and Bill was the *attendant* this time. I was driving fast that day, living up to the nickname they had given me. My mates called me "Fangio" after Juan Manuel Fangio, the famous Argentinian F1 racing driver of the 1950s. I always drove fast to incidents, and Bill was always saying, "Take your time, no rush." But I always wanted to get to the job first, as quickly as possible, and then take my time if necessary once I was there.

For that call, we arrived at the location but there was nothing there that would indicate a road accident had occurred. As Bill was checking the details of the call, a lady came to us with some information. It seems that a cyclist had come into contact with a car, but nobody was hurt and they had both left the scene some time ago. Mystery solved.

"Foxtrot 1, base, over."

"Base to Foxtrot 1, over."

"Foxtrot 1, not required at the RTA, nobody here, both the car and cyclist have left the scene, over."

"Roger Foxtrot 1, return to station, over."

"Roger, Foxtrot 1, over."

"Base out."

We arrived back on station at 2115 hrs and to my delight, we were last out. As I was getting ready to leave the station for the last time, I was given good wishes by most of the ambulancemen which was nice. My mate Bill wished me well and hoped I would find what I wanted at my new service. He also said that I should continue to be a "doctor" as he called it, but this time he said it more with a kind of pride because he was finally understanding my point of view.

That was the end of my service with Manchester Ambulance Service and I would soon be starting my new job in Cheadle Hulme. I thought back on all I had seen, from my first big event with the Green Man to the poor baby who had been so severely scalded. I wondered what awaited me at my new station, what kind of workmates I would have, what kind of career I would make for myself there.

Little did I know that my service with them would start off with so many bodies and body parts all in one week! In my wildest dreams, I couldn't have imagined a start like what happened. Even my new mates were surprised by the chaos, but it's all part of not being able to guess what any given day will bring.

THE GREEN MAN | TRUE STORIES OF A PARAMEDIC FROM THE ROADSIDE

8. Harrowing Week of Bodies and Body Parts

I didn't know exactly the flow of work or shifts because different services could set things up the way they wanted and the way it worked for them. I tried to be ready for anything when I arrived for my first duty at my new service, Cheshire County Ambulance Service. I got there at 0730 hrs. My duty was 0800 to 1800 on that day only, because I was new to the station and new to the area. Like an orientation day sort of, and I would find out during that day what my duties would be for the rest of the week.

I was met by the night crews and at Cheadle Hulme, there were two crews on the night shift which ran from 2000 hrs to 0800 hrs. I was introduced to the crews — Stan Green, Arnold Jackson, Ray Black and John Strines. They were really pleased to see me and told me that they thought that I would be working with Geoff Maynard.

I was shown where to sign on duty. There was no clocking on or off at this new place. Then it was up into the Mess Room. At about 0745 hrs, the rest of the staff started to arrive and one by one, I was introduced to them. There was a lot of good humoured banter about the Manchester Ambulance Service getting rid of their men who had been to Training School and sending them to the Cheshire stations. Just then the Sub Officer, Mike Jones, whom I had met when I visited the station previously, walked into the room.

"Hi Kid, I heard that you were starting today. Welcome and I hope that you will be very happy here!"

"Thank you, I am sure I will. These fellas seem full of fun."

"Don't leave any food lying about or it will be eaten," he cautioned with a good-humoured smile. "You can leave cash and nobody will touch it — just don't leave food."

He then got down to business. "I think you are working with Geoff Maynard today. I will let you know during the day what shifts you will be working for the rest of the week. Do you mind doing overtime?"

"No, I don't mind overtime at all."

The chatter continued and as different people came into the kitchen to make their tea or coffee, everbody was very pleasant. They each stopped to chat with me. I felt like a celebrity!

Then I heard: "Hi, you must be Ron. I'm Geoff Maynard." Geoff was about thirty-eight and he had a happy disposition.

"Pleased to meet you, Geoff," I said as I shook his hand.

"We are the *stand-by* crew this morning so do you want to come and check the equipment over with me?" he offered. "That way you will know where everything is."

If you are a *stand-by* crew, you answer all emergency calls.

I explained to Geoff that I did not know the area and then as we checked the equipment, I thought, this is like being in another world. They had masses of equipment. Geoff went over some of the kit that I had not seen since Wrenbury Hall and ensured that I was OK with it all. He also explained the radio procedure that was in use throughout Cheshire. It was a colour code system that is very important to use correctly.

Here's how it worked. If the crew was available for a call, they were said to be *green*. If they had non-urgent patients on board, their state was *blue* and if we were engaged in or on an emergency call, then the state was *red*.

There was also a code for the category of patients. It was called the "DU-MAS" code and it seemed very confusing when I first heard it but it became routine after a couple of days. We used it all the time.

Code 1 = **D**ead

Code 2 = **U**nresponsive

Code 3 = **M**aternity

Code 4 = **A**ssault (could be on a patient or the crew)

Code 5 = **S**uicide

As we walked back across the yard into the station, crews were coming out to go on routine work. They were all happy and I thought how different this feeling was compared to that which I had been used to.

It was 0810 hrs and I was half-way up the stairs when there was a sudden ear piercing ringing of a very loud bell for about ten seconds. *What the hell is that for I thought?* Geoff who was ahead of me went into the Control Room and as I got to the top of the stairs he was sprinting towards me.

"A three-nines, collapse, Alderley Edge," he said quickly. A three-nines is a 999 call — same as a 911 — so I hustled after him. As we ran across to the ambulance bay, I asked Geoff where Alderley Edge was.

"It is about seven miles away, so not too far," he said. He told me the call sign of the ambulance we had that day, it was Quebec 3, and he told me how to book mobile. This was new to me, but I did as he asked.

"Quebec 3 to base, red to Alderley Edge, over."

"Quebec 3, roger that, 0812, base out."

We had a lot of traffic and the roads were fairly narrow but our ambulance had a very large blue light on the roof and blue lights on the front. We also had flashing headlights and two-tone horns. This is a proper service I thought as we punched our way through traffic. Geoff was not saying much other than shouting above the deafening noise in the cab from the horns and the engine to tell me that I also needed to tell Control when we arrived on scene. Geoff told me that we were almost on scene and to call Control.

"Quebec 3 to base, at scene, over."

"Roger Quebec 3, 0826, base out."

We both jumped out of the ambulance and went into the house. The patient was a man in his sixties and he had clearly suffered a stroke. We asked his wife about his normal health and how long had he been like he was at that moment. She told us that this had happened around 0800 and she had called us straight away. The patient was unresponsive and his breathing sounded like he was snoring. Geoff suggested that we establish his airway and get him into the ambulance.

Geoff went for the equipment and in a flash he returned with a carry chair, blankets and disposable airways. He asked in a very quiet voice if I was OK inserting the airway. I asked him to do it which he did. In an instant, the airway was in place and the patient's breathing improved. We loaded him into the ambulance and I set up the oxygen. Geoff asked me which hospital I would like to go to and what sort of drive did I want! I was bewildered. I had no idea where I was, so I just asked for a fairly fast, smooth drive.

"OK, but which hospital?" he said.

"I have no idea. What do you suggest?" I asked.

"Macclesfield is nearest, only about six miles away. I'll go there." I had no idea, but apparently in Cheshire, the attendant in the back of the ambulance decides which hospital to go to and the speed of the journey. We set off for Macclesfield with blue lights and two-tones when necessary.

"Quebec 3 to base, red to Macclesfield, Code 2, over."

"Roger Quebec 3, 0841, base out.

Geoff had called Control while I worked on the patient. He was still unresponsive but making some very slight movements. How much further to the hospital I thought? All I could see through the darkened glass windows were fields. Then suddenly, we were coming into a town. I wondered if this was Macclesfield and sure enough, it was.

Just a couple of minutes later, we arrived at Macclesfield Infirmary.

"Quebec 3, red at Macclesfield, over.

"Roger Quebec 3, 0852, base out."

Geoff helped get the man out of the ambulance using the stretcher trolley. Cheshire ambulances had stretchers with wheels. Then off we went into the casualty department, and clearly Geoff was well known. Most of the nurses seemed to know him for sure.

I did a detailed handover and afterwards, Geoff introduced me to various nurses and members of the staff. All the smiles and formalities over with, we went on a tour of the various departments. Resuscitation Room (Resus), Plaster Room, X-Ray and finally into what looked like a small training room.

"Wow, is this the staff training area?" I asked.

"Yes. Do you want to renew your skills with OPAs?" asked Geoff. "We're allowed to use it if we need to, so now is a good time to practise." Within a couple of minutes my confidence was transformed and I had my skills back again.

"We use a lot of OPAs because our patients are in the ambulance for quite a while," said Geoff.

"Thanks very much Geoff, that was a huge help," I told him. "I had only used OPAs on a training dummy at Wrenbury but that was last May."

"Any more OPAs that we might need today, *you* can do them," he said.

Geoff then showed me how to complete the paperwork and with that done, it was time to call Control.

"Quebec 3 to base, over."

"Base, Quebec 3, over"

"Quebec 3, green at Macclesfield Infirmary, over."

"Roger Quebec 3, return to station, 0922. Can you come back along the A523, over?"

I looked at Geoff not knowing what that message meant. "Just say roger and I will explain to you," he said.

"Quebec 3, roger, over."

"Base out."

Geoff explained that road numbers were used a lot by Control and since there were two very different ways of returning the seventeen miles back to station, today the Control Room wanted us to return along the A523 road. We rolled into station at 1008 hrs and I booked us back.

"Quebec 3, base, over."

"Base, Quebec 3, over."

"Quebec 3, green on station, over."

"Base out."

As we walked into the station, Mick Jones, the Sub Officer, met us.

"How was your first emergency call with Cheshire?" he said.

"Not like Manchester, it was great!" I told him.

"How was he, Geoff? Does he need *training* into our ways?" Mick asked.

"Not at all," he said. "He is raring to get stuck into anything I think."

That was the only emergency call that day although we did do a few urgent admissions in the afternoon. My shift finished at 1800 that first day but I was told that the next day it would be 0800 hrs to 2000 hrs, and I would be working with Ray Black. He was on his days off so I had not met him yet, but everybody assured me that we would get on well.

Although I had only just started at Cheadle Hulme Station, I quickly picked up the routine. I arrived for work at 0735 hrs and met the same night crew as the day before. We chatted about how I had found my first day and about their fairly busy night. A couple of people whom I had already met came into the Mess Room and the chatter continued. Then a distinguished looking man with hair that looked like a badger, white at the sides and black on top came in. I was introduced to him. His name was Ray Black.

"Yes, I met you a couple of months ago when I visited the station while I was at Wrenbury Hall," I said to him.

"Oh, did we meet, I don't recall," he replied.

"I think I am working with you today, Ray," I said.

"Yes, we are, and I usually have a quiet shift."

We chatted for a few minutes and then he disappeared over to the ambulance bays. I went down and found him checking an ambulance. This ambulance looked fairly new and it was painted white, a colour that was being tested to see if the vehicle stood out more than the cream colour of the others. It was also an automatic, something that was almost unheard of in 1969.

Besides the colour change, I admired the automatic gearbox and the single wide backdoor instead of two doors. It also had two stretcher trolleys, one of which could be elevated to various heights. I noticed that its number plate was "F 111 XTU" and it was known by crews as the "F111" (pronounced F-one-eleven) after the American fighter aircraft. They named it that because apparently it would fly along. I helped Ray finish checking the ambulance and I familiarised myself where everything was stowed.

Back in the Mess Room after everybody else had gone out, we chatted about Manchester Ambulance and why I wanted to work for Cheshire. Ray had also worked for Manchester until ten years ago and he had transferred because this station was nearer to where he lived. As we talked together, a typical summer thunderstorm started, rain so heavy it was like a fog, accompanied by lightening and severe thunder. We stood by the window watching the downpour and the lightening, being thankful that we were not out in it.

At 1000 hrs exactly, the bells rang long and loud. Ray grabbed the ticket from the Control Room and as he caught up with me going down the stairs he said, "Three people struck by lightning, off Cheadle Road." Ray jumped into the driving seat, started up and off we went.

"What is our call sign, Ray?"

"Quebec 1."

"Quebec 1, red to Cheadle Road."

"Roger Quebec 1, 1001, base out."

Ray had the two-tones blasting away and since there was very little traffic we were at the scene very quickly.

"Quebec 1, red at scene, over."

"Roger Quebec 1, 1003, base out."

It was still pouring with rain and thundering, but the lightening had moved away, thank goodness. We were met by a man with a golf cart, but he was the other side of a fence. I climbed over the fence and heard the man was telling us that this was really bad. Ray passed me over some equipment, including the Minuteman Resuscitator, blankets, and airways. Ray decided to stay with the ambulance while I did an assessment.

The golf cart bumped along to a group of trees about 100 yards away. As we approached, I could see three people lying on the ground and they all looked bluish in the face. A bluish colour in the face is usually a sign of cardiac arrest and the heart has stopped. *This can't be three bodies, can it, I thought?*

As I jumped off the golf cart, I saw that it was indeed what appeared to be three bodies. The one in the centre had his head and face split wide open and his trousers were burned near his right trouser pocket. I had never seen a head split in half before. I quickly checked the other two but they were all dead. *Bloody hell, I thought, what am I supposed to do now?* I asked the golf cart man to go back to the road where the ambulance was parked and ask my mate Ray to call another crew and then to come over and help me.

In the meantime, I was attempting to resuscitate at least one of the patients but it was a lost cause. I examined all three and the man with the split head also had burns to the back of his head. He had clearly been struck by a bolt of lightning. They were all next to a tree which was split part way down the trunk.

Ray finally arrived and we set about preparing to move the bodies. Shortly afterwards, another two crews arrived and after about an hour we had all three bodies in the ambulances and the convoy was ready to set off.

"Is Stockport Infirmary OK, Ron it's about six miles away."

"Yes, thanks, Ray."

"Quebec 1 to base, over."

"Base Quebec 1, over."

"Quebec 1, red to Stockport Infirmary, Code 1 over."

"Roger Quebec 1, can you confirm three DOAs, over."

"Quebec 1, roger, we have one Code 1, Tango 1 and Romeo 1 have a Code 1 each, over."

"Roger, base out."

Whenever there is a fatality involved, the ambulance service informs the police, and they then tell the relatives.

Ray suddenly said, "You're a bloody jinx, aren't you? Three for the price of one. Were you a jinx at Manchester?"

"I'm not a jinx, it just looks like that," I told him.

"Did you get a lot of multiple patients from jobs in Manchester?" he asked.

"A few, but never on a golf course," I replied.

All three ambulances arrived at the hospital at the same time and I followed Ray into the casualty department. He introduced me to the few nurses that were there and we explained what we had brought in. A doctor came out to certify our body with the split head and commented that he had never seen that type of injury from lightening before.

Then he looked at the burn on patient's leg and although it was not very deep, the doctor pulled out of the burned pocket a small lump of metal which had been coins until they melted when the current from the lightening exited his body. All this happened while the three of them were leaning on the tree for shelter.

From the hospital, we went over to the police mortuary, again in a convoy and of course we attracted a lot of attention from the Police Station personnel who were curious to see three ambulances arriving at the same time at the mortuary.

Eventually we were finished and cleaned up and Ray again commented about me being a jinx.

"Call Control and ask for more bodies," quipped Ray.

"Be careful what you wish for, Ray." I felt that his banter was light-hearted and said in fun, his way to diffuse some of the trauma we had just encountered.

"Quebec 1 to base, over."

"Base, Quebec 1, over."

"Quebec 1, green at the mortuary, over."

"Roger Quebec 1, return to station 1216, over."

"Quebec 1, roger, over."

"Base out."

We arrived back on station at around 1245 hrs and I was ready for my lunch. I suddenly thought about the first time I had been in a mortuary a couple of years ago with the Green Man and how I had not wanted to eat afterwards. Things were much different these days. I could face anything now or so I thought.

When lunch was over, Ray and I chatted for a while. Mick, the Sub

Officer, came into the Mess Room and made some coffee. We all sat there with our cups and Ray was telling Mick about the three bodies.

"Bloody hell, did they teach you that at Wrenbury?" he blurted out.

"Teach me what?" I said.

"How to get bodies in bulk!"

Without warning, the bells went. I was out of the door first and into the Control Room.

"Hi Ron, another golf club job for you. Ray will know where that is."

I sprinted out to the ambulance and gave Ray the emergency sheet. "A collapse in the gents' toilet, Bramhall Park Golf Club."

"Quebec 1, red to Bramhall Golf Club, over."

"Roger Quebec 1, 1325, Base out."

Ray just looked across at me with a disbelieving look on his face.

"How can you do this to me? Another bloody golf course. I hate golf!"

"It's not me," I protested as we hurtled along.

This really is like the Phantom F111, I thought. It really does go fast!

"Quebec 1, red at scene, over."

"Roger Quebec 1, 1335, Base out."

I jumped out and I was shown where the patient was. The Gentlemen's Toilet was on the ground floor and as I walked in, there were a couple of people there.

"Hello, what has happened?" I said.

"We just found him in here. He really doesn't look well," somebody said.

I am not surprised, he doesn't look well, I thought to myself, he's bloody dead.

"How long has he been here like this?" I asked them.

"About twenty minutes. We were trying to get him to speak."

"Oh, was he conscious when you first saw him?"

"No, just as he is now."

"Well, does he have any relatives here with him in the club?"

"No, but his friend Dr. Simpson came to see him and told us that he had passed away."

"Where is Dr. Simpson now?"

"He's left the club now."

"OK, we will move him to Stockport Infirmary and then to the mortuary."

I went outside and told Ray what the situation was, and he looked bemused at the information.

"Are you sure you're not a bloody *undertaker* in disguise?"

We took our trolley into the toilet and loaded the patient onto it. Out into the ambulance and after getting information from the club staff regarding the details of the patient, we set off to Stockport Infirmary and to the mortuary — again!

"Quebec 1, Base, over."

"Base, Quebec 1, over."

"Quebec 1, red to Stockport Infirmary, Code 1 over.

"Roger Quebec 1, 1350, Base out."

Ray was now in his element joking about how I must be an undertaker *in real life* as he put it, but it was all in fun and there was no animosity at all. Finally after certification, we were cleaned up at the mortuary and ready to go.

"Quebec 1, Base, over."

"Base, Quebec 1, over."

"Quebec 1, green at Stockport Mortuary, over."

"Roger, Quebec 1. I have an emergency for you. Attend a collapse at the sixteenth tee, Bramhall Golf Club on Ladythorne Road, Bramhall. Confirming this is *not* Bramhall Park Golf Club where you have just been. Time to you is 1456, over."

"Quebec 1, Roger over."

"This might be number five," I said to Ray.

"Are you always like this?" asked Ray?

"Like what?" I said.

It was too noisy for any more normal conversation in the cab and Ray was concentrating on driving. The location of this golf club was about five miles away and there was the start of traffic building up which of course made driving difficult.

Finally, Ray said that we were approaching the golf club, but he pointed out that we were not at the scene. The scene was on the Sixteenth Tee!

"Quebec 1, Base over."

"Base, Quebec 1, over."

"Quebec 1, red at Bramhall Golf Club, over."

"Roger Quebec 1, 1512, base out."

We were approached by a man on a big golf cart and he told us that the patient was receiving CPR from another golfer. We asked him to lead the way and we would follow in the ambulance.

"You can't drive that damn thing onto the golf course," he protested. "Load your equipment onto this cart and I will take it."

"What about us? How do we get there?" asked Ray.

I suggested to Ray that I would go on the golf cart and see if he could organise another for the equipment.

"Good idea," said Ray so off I went to the sixteenth tee which seemed miles away. The patient was blue but CPR was being done in a fashion.

"How long since he collapsed?" I asked.

"About twenty-five minutes" said a golfer standing nearby.

"Let me just do a quick check, please." I checked the airway and listened for breathing.

The airway was full of vomit, quite often caused by well-meaning bystanders pressing in the wrong place when doing chest compressions. I cleared the vomit out as best as I could by turning the patient onto his side and sweeping out his mouth and throat. Just as I was finishing that, Ray arrived on a golf cart with lots of equipment.

We set to work with the Minuteman Resuscitator which was a "positive pressure ventilator" that also had a small suction unit built in. The airway was now clear and I inserted an OPA in order to keep the tongue off the back of his throat.

Ray was using the Minuteman and I was doing compressions. We knew that this was useless, but we were trying. Ray had managed to get the trolley across the greens on the golf cart, so we loaded the patient onto it and I balanced on the top in order to continue CPR. We sped off towards the ambulance and Ray recruited some help with getting the patient on the trolley off the cart. Once inside the ambulance, I connected the patient to the main oxygen supply and continued CPR.

"Quebec 1 to Base, over."

"Base, Quebec 1, over."

"Quebec 1, red to Stockport, over."

"Roger Quebec 1, 1541, Base out."

And so, we were heading for Stockport Infirmary once more.

"Quebec 1, red at Stockport, over."

"Roger Quebec 1, 1553, Base out."

As we arrived at the casualty department, one of our other crews was already there and as Ray got out, I heard them ask what the job was.

"Another bloody body — number bloody five today," Ray told them.

"Did you say five today? Who's in the back?"

"*The Undertaker*, yes, five. You know, the new fella, Ron. He attracts bodies like flies to shit! It's a bloody record for our station. Nobody has ever had five bodies in one day!"

Ray opened the back door and asked if we were taking the body in or did we want the doctor to come out? I asked for the doctor to come out as the patient was clearly deceased. I jumped out and had a chat with the other crew who told me that Ray usually had very quiet shifts. I just smiled and said that today must be his unlucky day.

Ray came out of the casualty department with the same doctor that had certified our other four bodies and as the doctor passed me to climb into the ambulance, he just said, "What time does your shift finish?"

"2000," I replied.

"Well, you have time for another four bodies then, don't you?" the doctor said darkly. He had a look of complete incredulity as he examined the body.

"Thank you, doctor, but I think that will be the end of bodies today," I told him.

"I hope so, I don't want to see either of you again today." And with that comment he was on his way back into the Casualty Department.

We delivered our body to the mortuary, completed all our paperwork and we were ready for work again.

"I have never had a day like this. Really, I usually have a relaxing shift," claimed Ray.

"Well, I am finding this amount of fatal collapses and the lightning strike job amazing," I said. "Jimmy Richards at Wrenbury was right when he said how busy it is at Cheadle Hulme, but he also said that there are plenty of bad jobs that you can get your teeth into."

Ray took another perspective. "Well, jobs *to get your teeth into* seem to have evaded you, all you have had today are bloody bodies!"

"Quebec 1 to Base, over"

"Base, Quebec 1, over"

"Quebec 1, green at Stockport mortuary, over."

"Roger Quebec 1, return to station, 1640, Base out."

It was a busy time on the roads now but Ray knew some short cuts which allowed us to miss a lot of stationary traffic.

"Base, Quebec 1, urgent over."

"What the bloody hell do they want now?" said Ray.

"Quebec 1, green almost at station, over."

"Base, Quebec 1, I have an emergency for you."

"Quebec 1, roger, pass the details, over."

"Quebec 1, attend a collapse at Hazel Grove Golf Course, Buxton Road, Hazel Grove, 1700, over."

"Quebec 1, roger."

"Base, Quebec 1, if I get a nearer mobile, I will stop you. Base out."

"I don't bloody believe it. This cannot be happening," said Ray. He was glaring at me as thought I was making people collapse.

"Do you know where this golf club is?" he asked.

"I have no idea, Ray, where is it?"

"It's about seven miles away and in evening traffic it will take us a good twenty minutes."

I just sat there wondering to myself what had attracted all these collapses today.

Ray was trying to fight through the traffic but in some cases, we just could not get through. After a nightmare drive, Ray finally got us to the club.

"Quebec 1, red at the golf club, over."

"Roger Quebec 1, 1718, base out."

The actual club house was well off the main road and as we approached it, there were people waving and the appearance of panic. They were clearly waving at us to hurry up.

I jumped out and was instantly met with aggression from a couple of big men who grabbed the front of my shirt. "Where in the bloody hell have you been? We called over half an hour ago."

"Let go of me or I will call the police and have you arrested for assault," I assured him.

Reluctantly he let go and gave me a push as he did so. We were there for an emergency, not a fight.

"What are we here for?" I asked.

"A member has collapsed at the fifth and a doctor is doing CPR, so get a bloody move on."

Then, without warning somebody grabbed my arm and started pulling me.

"Let go now! What's wrong with you people?" I said.

"Come on, hurry up."

"How am we supposed to get all our equipment to the patient? Have you got a couple of golf carts?" I asked.

"We should have taken him by golf cart. We would have been quicker than you lot."

"Do you know where we have come from?" I asked.

 "The Ambulance Station just down the road I suppose."

"We have come from Cheadle Hulme and we received the call at 1700, so shut up and get us to the patient," I told them, in no uncertain terms.

Two golf carts arrived, and Ray and I loaded them up with equipment. We were taken out to the fifth tee where a few people were standing around looking down at the patient on the ground.

"Hello sir. How long have you been doing CPR?"

"Hello, I'm Dr. Thompson and he is well beyond reviving," came the reply.

"Thanks for waiting for us. Can you tell us what happened please?"

"He is one of my patients and I have been seeing him recently with severe chest pains," the doctor shared. "He has had three MIs and as we were teeing off, he just dropped to the ground. I think he was dead before he hit the ground. I tried resuscitation but it is a waste of time, no need for you to try."

"Thank you, doctor. We will take him to Stockpot Infirmary and then onto the mortuary."

"Thank you, boys."

I asked the doctor for his details and as much information about the deceased man as he could tell us.

We went through the same routine as the last DOA and eventually we got him into the ambulance.

"You are a bloody *undertaker*," Ray insisted. "I don't know any crew who has had six bodies in one day. It's is a record that will stand for years."

"Quebec 1 to Base over."

"Base, Quebec 1, over"

"Quebec 1, red to Stockport, another DOA, over."

There was silence and then, "Quebec 1, roger, 1726. Do you also sell coffins by any chance?"

"My mate thinks I'm an undertaker."

"Roger Quebec 1, so do we, base out."

As we were approaching Stockport Infirmary, I called the Control Room.

"Quebec 1, red at Stockport, over.

"Roger Quebec 1, 1759 base out."

Ray told me to go into the department and find a doctor. He said that he was too embarrassed to go and ask for a doctor yet again. As I walked in I saw "our" same doctor talking to a nurse. Suddenly he saw me and with a look of dread on his face, he came over.

"Hello doctor. Please could you certify a body for us?"

"Are you serious or is this a joke?"

"I am serious, another body off a golf course I'm afraid," I told him.

"Golf doesn't seem to be a healthy sport, does it?" he said with a resigned voice.

So the same procedure as before and soon we were on the way to the mortuary.

"Quebec 1 to Base, over."

"Base, Quebec 1, over."

"Quebec 1, green at the mortuary, over."

"Roger Quebec 1, return to station, 1822, Base out."

We finally arrived on station at 1840 hrs and made a coffee, our first since lunchtime. Different officers from the Control Room came in to see who had been getting all the bodies. One officer, Andy Murphy, thanked us for our work and promised no more bodies tomorrow.

Ray looked exhausted after all that work but he did say how much he enjoyed the day working with me and of course, the feeling was mutual. So that was the end of my second day: six bodies by one crew in one day from different golf courses was a record. It's a record which as far as I know still stands today.

Time to sleep, time to get up. Off to my third day.

"Good morning, Ray," I said when I got in.

"Morning Ron. Are we working together again today?" he asked.

"I think so, provided that I read the crew list correctly."

Ray looked at the list and confirmed that we were indeed a crew again today.

"I do not want another day like yesterday, no bodies today," he warned me.

"I'll see what I can do."

The atmosphere on the station was like being on holiday. Despite the many strange calls, everybody was happy, the area that we covered was very varied, and it was a really nice station to work in. Other crews were arriving for work and they all were saying "good morning" to each other. A few asked if I was the *body man* that they had heard about?

After checking over our ambulance, the F111, we made some coffee and started to chat about a wide variety of subjects. Ray asked me when I went to Training School and if I enjoyed it. I told him that I was there in May, and how much I enjoyed it and I asked him when he last went.

"We have to go every two years. It's mandatory in Cheshire."

"Really, every two years?" I said.

"That has been Cheshire's policy for many years. We are all trained the same way. If you go to another station, say Runcorn for example, which is around forty-five miles away but still a Cheshire station, they work the same way that we do."

We went on to chat about holidays, cars and aircraft. Our station was on the final approach into Manchester International Airport. Aircraft were about six hundred feet up as they passed by around a half mile away. Ray was a keen *aircraft spotter* and he knew his subject well. He also had a portable radio tuned to the aircraft and air traffic control frequencies. It was interesting to watch the aircraft go by and listen to their conversations.

The day was very quiet, just three urgent admissions to hospital and nothing else. By late afternoon, I was thoroughly bored, and we still had a few hours to go until finishing time at 2000. I checked the crew list for the next day and I was working with somebody called Stan Green. I had not met him yet and I wondered what he was like to work with. Finally, after a very quiet day, my shift came to an end. I hoped that tomorrow would be a more interesting day and yes, it did turn out that way.

So Day Four was my last day of working of my first week and I was working with Stan Green. I did not know Stan but I had heard about him. He was about six foot three and a couple of years older than I was. He had been born and bred in the area and he knew *everybody*. As he walked into the Mess Room, I presumed that this man must be him. He had a jolly look on his face and a warm smile.

Somebody said to him, "Hi Stan, how was the camp?" Stan was the leader of a local Boy Scout Troop and they had been away in the country for a week camping.

"It was good apart from the rain, three days solid and no let up," he described. "We were soaked!"

Stan was looking at me in a strange way — as though he knew me. Then he said, "Are you the new fella from Manchester?"

"Yes, my name is Ron Gillatt."

We shook hands and it must have looked funny me being short and Stan being so tall. There were lots of comments about that and lots of laughter.

"You won't laugh in a minute, Stan," a voice rang out. "He had six bodies on Tuesday with Ray, so Ray has christened him the undertaker!"

"Six, in one day?"

"Yes. And ask him where they were from."

"Off golf courses," I said.

"Same golf course or different ones?"

"Three off one, and three off three different ones!"

"Ray must have been going mad," said Stan. "Has he ever had that many bodies — apart from a major incident?"

Just then Mick came into the Mess Room and started to get the crews out to their ambulances.

"Hi Stan, have you met Ron?" Mick said.

"Yes, I believe he is the station *undertaker* now?"

"Well, today he is your *undertaker*. He is working with you today on the F111."

A look of resignation came over Stan's face and with that, we went out to check the ambulance.

"Do you want to drive this morning and I'll drive this afternoon?" asked Stan.

"I don't mind," I said. "I have not driven yet and that is mainly because I just don't know the area yet."

"No problems there," said Stan. "I will talk you through where to go if we get a job and if necessary, you take over attending and I will drive."

"That sounds perfect. I appreciate that."

We checked the vehicle from front to back and top to bottom. Stan was very thorough and when we were done, we went back into the station.

"Do you know where the spare equipment is and how to book it out?" Stan asked me.

"No, I don't," I said. "Do we need something that is missing?"

"We need a couple of burn dressings, a disposable oxygen mask and some heavy-duty plastic bags."

"What are the bags for?" I asked.

"They are for a number of different uses, mainly for lying on or kneeling on the roadside or in a field or anywhere it is really dirty," said Stan. "They are very thick and strong. We carry ten bags in the rescue kit."

We got the spares and I took them out to the ambulance while Stan made a coffee. We sat and chatted for quite a while and without warning, Stan said, "I have seen you before, I am sure of it."

"Oh, where and when? Sorry to say, Stan, but I don't think I have met you before."

"It was a while ago. You brought an RTA into the Manchester Royal Infirmary — a motorcyclist with two open femurs."

"Ah, yes, I remember the job but I do not remember seeing you. What a memory."

We chatted about the Boy Scouts and Stan's camping trip. He had taken the troop up into the hills in Derbyshire, a beautiful area but it catches a lot of rain.

1120 hrs and the bells rang out.

"I'll get the ticket, Ron," said Stan.

"OK, I'll get the motor running," I said quickly.

"Somebody hit by a train in Bramhall. Go to the railway station and the Transport Police will walk us up the line to the impact point."

Stan grabbed the radio and booked us mobile.

"Quebec 1, red to Bramhall, over."

"Base, Quebec 1, roger, 1121, base out."

Bloody hell, I thought, I have never had somebody knocked down by a train before.

"Which way, Stan?" I asked as I jumped up into the driver's seat. Stan talked me through to the station about five miles away. The drive was fast and smooth, and I thought, this F111 really does get a move on when you want it to.

As we arrived at the train station, we were met by the police who informed us that this was a fatal and all the trains were halted until they would complete their investigation.

"Quebec 1, red at Bramhall Station, over."

"Roger, 1128, base out."

"Grab some of those plastic bags, Ron," said Stan with a confident voice.

"OK, how many?" I asked.

"Bring four, I think that should be enough."

I grabbed four of the bags and then we followed the police officer along the track towards a group of railway staff and police. We then had a briefing by the police who told us that the rear of the train that was in the distance was the London to Manchester express and it usually travelled through Bramhall Station at around 100 miles per hour. Apparently, it was the impact of this train that had caused the fatality we were attending. I thought I was ready for anything, but what came next from the policeman was still a shock.

"Don't look for a body, lads, look for *bits* of a body," he said gravely.

I looked at Stan. Was the policeman serious about *us* looking for bits of a body?

"OK, thanks, do you want to do all that side, Ron, and I'll do all this side?" said Stan.

"Are we really looking for bits of body?" I said in a low voice, still a bit confused and hoping I had not heard the instructions correctly.

"Yes. Have you not done this before?" asked Stan.

"No. I have never had a body on the railway line before."

"Oh, sorry Ron, I didn't know that. This is a shitty start for you on this type of job," said Stan.

"What we do is walk along the track looking for body parts and collect them in the plastic bags. We also check in the grass and weeds at the side of the track. When we have more or less enough parts to make up to three quarters of a body, we take the parts to be certified and then to the mortuary."

What a grim task, I thought, but it was our job and we set off on the search for body parts, something that I had never thought would be part of my job. The pictures are still in my memory today as clear as yesterday. We gathered up what we could find. My last piece was part of the top lip and most of the nose. No piece was bigger than a hand. It was a nightmare job but eventually we had two bags of *bits*.

We walked back up the track into the station and over to the ambulance. We placed the bags onto the stretcher trolley and closed the door.

"Well, that was not a nice job," said Stan. "Did you not get many jobs like that in Manchester?"

"I suppose there might have been a few, but I never heard of anybody collecting body parts like this before," I admitted. "OK, let's get to Stockport."

"Quebec 1 to base over."

"Base, Quebec 1, over."

"Quebec 1, red to Stockport, confirming a DOA. Over."

"Quebec 1, did you have to collect, over."

"What does he mean, did we have to *collect*?" I asked Stan.

"They wanted to know if we had to collect the bits and pieces," said Stan.

"Quebec 1, roger to that, over,"

"Thank you, 1225, base out."

We travelled to Stockport in a steady but progressive way.

"Quebec 1, red at Stockport, over."

"Quebec 1, roger, 1242, base out."

We went through what had now become routine with me, certification followed by the mortuary and then clean up. Finally, after everything was completed, Stan called the control.

"Quebec 1 to base, over."

"Base, Quebec 1, over."

"Quebec 1, green at Stockport Mortuary, over."

"Roger Quebec 1, return to station, 1318, base out."

We arrived back on station at 1340 and replenished the supply of plastic bags before heading up to have lunch. Over our lunch we discussed the job we had just done. It was around the *Mess Room* table that so many horror situations had always been discussed. Most ambulance crews never told their families about what they had experienced during a shift. I know I didn't. Families could not possibly understand what it is like to deal with the work that is almost mind-numbingly sad to ambulance crews. The only people who understand what you go through on a daily basis are other emergency service workers.

We owe a huge debt to the Mess Room table. It is impartial, non-judgmental and it never says "*I know how you feel.*"

The rest of the shift was fairly routine with three relatively minor emergencies and that being my last shift of the week, I wondered what the following weeks, months and years would bring?

9. Life Goes On – For Some

It seemed like just a flash the day I suddenly realized that I had been with Cheshire Ambulance Service for over a year. Although the serious calls still came in, they became almost predictable and of course, I was then familiar with the area. I had also become more confident in trying to adapt different methods of treatment to a variety of different injuries.

Some things changed at Cheadle Hulme Ambulance Station in that first year. We had some staff transfer to other stations and other people transfer in. A new station had been built some miles away and ten of our staff had transferred to that new location. That left us with fourteen people including our two Sub Officers. What this meant to us on a day-to-day basis was that most people were crewed up with one of two people depending where they were on the crew list.

I had two people with whom I worked. Ray Black and Stan Green were my two partners. We got on very well with each other and that made the job so much easier.

I was on night shift with Ray on Quebec 3 on a cold November Saturday night. The evening was fairly quiet and we had only done a stand-by at an ambulance station that covered the M6 Motorway at a town called Knutsford. This station was about twenty miles from our station and no sooner had we arrived when we were released and we returned to our own station.

I was going for a week of *hospital training* on Monday morning so I hoped that the weekend nights would be quiet. Hospital training involved working in the Casualty Department, the Coronary Care Unit, and in the operating theatre. It was very intensive, and you were part of the team with all the responsibilities that go along with that role. I loved training. The more the better for me and so I was really looking forward to it. I had been studying very hard so I would be prepared.

At 0217 the bells went and the call was to a house fire about two miles away. Since the fire station was adjoining the ambulance station, we heard their bells go at about the same time as ours.

"Quebec 3 to base, red to Cheadle, over."

"Quebec 3, roger, 0218, base out."

As we turned out onto the main road, the fire appliances were just nosing out of their station. We were going to an address in a residential area and a fire call at that time of night was usually going to be something rather than nothing.

We arrived at scene and we parked well past the address in order to allow the fire crews the closest access.

"Quebec 3 to base, red at scene, over."

"Roger Quebec 3, 0223, base out."

The fire turned out to be a garden rubbish fire that was thought to have been extinguished by the home owner before they went to bed. A neighbour had woken up to the smell of smoke and called the fire brigade. It turned out that we were not required at the scene and as we left, we wished the firemen a quiet rest of the night.

"Quebec 3 to base over."

"Base, Quebec 3, over."

"Quebec 3, green in Cheadle, not required, just a garden rubbish fire, over."

"Roger Quebec 3, return to station, 0240, over."

"Quebec 3, roger."

"Base out."

A few minutes later we were back on station and thinking about a coffee and feet up time. But not for long. At 0306 hrs, the bells went off. I grabbed the ticket from Harry Warren in the Control Room.

"This sounds like a bad one, Ron, A34 and Finney Lane, Heald Green. Two cars head on and one of them is about eighty yards away from the other. Sounds like a real mess," he said.

I ran down the stairs and Ray already had the ambulance at the door, I gave him the details and booked mobile.

"Quebec 3, red to the RTA, over."

"Roger Quebec 3, 0307, let me know if you need more crews."

"Roger will do."

It was a very fast trip. There was no traffic at that hour and no time to spare.

"Quebec 3 to base, red at scene, over."

"Roger Quebec 3, 0310, base out."

The road accident was about one and a half miles away and as we reached the junction where the accident was, it was bloody carnage. Debris and broken glass everywhere and two people trapped in the first car. Somebody was doing CPR on the driver who I very rapidly checked and realised through my experience that he was already dead.

I told the lady doing CPR that it was no good and she could help in other ways since it appeared that we had a lot of patients. She ignored me other than to accuse me of refusing to save the man's life because she knew he was still alive because of the noises that he was making. I told her he was dead and she should leave him and help others if she wanted to help. People sometimes make strange noises soon after dying.

I turned my head and saw a female passenger who was in a desperate state with a large amount of blood leaking from a severe leg injury and she was gasping for breath.

Ray had gone to assess the other vehicle and had come across two people lying in the roadway already dead due to non-survivable head injuries. I ran to the ambulance and called Control with a situation report.

"Quebec 3 to base, urgent, over."

"Base to Quebec 3, go ahead."

"Quebec 3, we have three Code 1's and five with multiple injuries, we need six more ambulances as quickly as possible, and the Fire Brigade, over."

"Roger, I will send Congleton (22 miles away), Macclesfield (17 miles away), Altrincham (12 miles away) and Knutsford (20 miles away). I will ask Manchester to send two, keep me in the picture, 0315, base out."

I returned to the first car that I had checked out and I found an off-duty policeman had stopped to help.

"Please could you be the runner between me and my colleague who is at the other car?" I asked him.

"No problem, what shall I tell him?"

"Tell him that we have six ambulances coming from different stations and also the fire brigade."

As I started treating the lady, I found that she had a pneumothorax which is a hole in the chest wall which was allowing air to enter her chest and potentially could collapse a lung and squash her heart. Tending to her was an absolute priority in saving her life. I sealed the hole as I had been taught at Training School and thought back to the time when there was no training. At that time, she would have died, there was no doubt about that. Almost immediately her breathing stabilised and since I also had her on oxygen, the improvement was significant.

Then I had to deal with the blood loss from the leg. She had a gaping wound stretching from mid-thigh to just below the knee and as I attempted to close the wound and control the bleeding, the first fire crew arrived. These were the firemen that we had been out to the garden fire with earlier and as the officer in charge asked how they could help, I asked if their second crew could go and help Ray.

Ray had three trapped in the other car which was about 70 yards away. They had relatively minor injuries, broken bones, lacerations and the stench of beer. It was a chaotic scene, lots of noise, people screaming in pain. Wherever you walked, you were crunching over broken glass, and it reminded me of walking along a beach covered in pebbles. We had a general feeling of helplessness as we waited for the patients to be cut out of their respective cars. There was only so much that we could do in the mangled wrecks.

The lady who had been doing CPR was finally moved by the police who were now arriving in numbers. The lady wanted to make a state-ment to the police accusing me of refusing to treat the patient that she claimed was alive when we arrived at the scene. This was a very serious accusation and the police took it seriously. I was cautioned that I would be interviewed at a later date.

I was not really very interested at that time in her accusation and the fact that I would be interviewed by the police. I was still busy trying to help the people we could help. The fire brigade was working on cutting the lady out of the car that I had been stabilising just as the first two extra ambulances crews arrived.

When I was at Training School, Jimmy Richards had said that my new station would have plenty of shitty jobs that you can get your teeth into. This really was one of those jobs and we had got our teeth into it. Within a few minutes I was glad to see that my lady was freed and I called one of the two ambulance crews over and asked them to move her. I gave them very detailed information regarding her injuries and away they went.

The three trapped people that Ray was dealing with were slowly being freed and as the first one was released, he was put straight into the other ambulance. He had suffered only a broken arm so he was very lucky. It seems he had been asleep and he thinks that he woke up on impact.

As they left, I took a moment to call Control with an update as to how things were progressing.

Soon afterwards, another ambulance arrived from Macclesfield and then Congleton arrived. It was now 0344. They must have had wings fitted, I thought, in order to get there so quickly.

Shortly afterwards, the last of the living were on their way to hospital, and this just left the dead bodies to be moved. The police photographer had been on scene for some time and had finished photographing the bodies by the time we were ready to move them.

The transporting of the bodies was fairly routine and one of the two extra ambulances that had arrived to help us efficiently loaded two bodies — one on each trolley. Ray and I loaded the driver who had received CPR.

"Quebec 3 to base, over."

"Base, Quebec 3, over.

"Quebec 3, red to Wythenshawe and then the mortuary, one male adult Code 1, over."

"Roger Quebec 1, 0435, base out."

We both went to Wythenshawe Hospital for certification and then over to their mortuary. We were filthy and covered in dried blood and general dirt, so it was time for a good wash.

Finally after we were clean once more and so was the ambulance, it was time to call Control.

"Quebec 3 to base over."

"Base, Quebec 3, over."

"Quebec 3, green at Wythenshawe Mortuary, over."

"Roger Quebec 3, return to station, 0520, base out."

It was a quiet ride back after such a long call and all the chaos.

"Quebec 3, green on station, over."

"Roger Quebec 3, base out."

It was Ray who drove us back and he was in a very sedate state. As soon as we arrived back on station, we were both suddenly hit by incredible sadness and fatigue. We both felt like having a good cry but we didn't do that. We were men after all.

However, after a cup of coffee and a chat around the Mess Room table between ourselves, a couple of firemen came in and we all sat there talking about the job that we had just been out on. I am just so thankful for that *Mess Room.* It was our salvation for a great many years. Almost every time we had a job, regardless of whether it was a bad job or a relatively routine job, we always sat around the table and discussed it. We would analyse every aspect of the job from starting off from the station to answer the call until we were back on station again.

We would discuss the drive to the job and comment on the frustration of how bad some drivers were and also how good some were. We all knew the feeling of the incredible noise in the cab with the engine roaring, the constant monotonous noise of the two-tone horns (the siren) and of course, we were always acutely aware of the time it was taking to get to the job.

We discussed our treatment of the patients we attended. Did we do everything that we should have done in the correct order? Did we do everything that we could or could we have done more? For us, the feeling of guilt was always lurking just waiting to pounce and together we could talk freely about it. Sometimes we did make small mistakes and sometimes we could have done things slightly differently, but we never made the patient worse. We were almost always able to improve their condition.

These debriefs at the table were like talking to somebody onto whom you could unburden yourself, someone who really knew how you might be feeling because they did the same job. By talking through the details, we were usually able to *keep the lid on* our emotions. Our debriefs made a difference because we were able to go home without the heavy burden of work and without being completely emotionally drained.

After chatting with us for about fifteen minutes, the firemen said that they felt the same as we did. They also filled us in on some more details we didn't know. They said the police told them that the car in which the three people were trapped had been involved in two other *failing to stop crashes* in a suburb of Manchester. Although the police had initially chased the car, they had called off the chase because of the danger to the public. Clearly the driver and passengers had all been drinking and finally, the influence of alcohol had killed three innocent people.

Then at 0630 hrs, two police officers arrived to interview me about the complaint made by the lady doing CPR. As if there was not enough stress from the RTA without dealing with all that on top of it, I thought.

While being interviewed, the police officers were polite, and I knew they had a job to do. Everything that I said in response to their questions was written down by the officer who was taking my statement.

"What was the condition of the patient who was receiving CPR when you arrived at the scene?" he began.

"Initially, I had to do a very rapid assessment as to how much help we would need." I explained. "Part of that assessment included judging the patient's condition, the one who was receiving CPR. I could clearly see the condition, and I told the lady delivering CPR that it was of no use because he was dead."

"Are you qualified to certify death?" he asked.

"No, but I am experienced enough to tell when somebody is dead," I said.

"Do you often tell relatives that their loved one is dead?" he asked.

"I didn't know that she was a relative, but he was dead."

"What do you usually say when you tell somebody that their, husband, wife, son, daughter or whoever is dead?" he asked.

"We use the term *signs of life are absent*," I explained. "That is as far as we can go."

"OK, so why did you not use that phrase when you told the lady that the patient was dead?" he asked.

"I did not have time for a discussion. I checked both carotid pulses which are the arteries either side of the neck, and from his colour which was bluish due to lack of oxygen and his massive chest injuries, I determined that signs of life were absent."

"OK, thanks Ron, sorry to put you through this but we have to follow up on complaints," he said. "You will have to go to Coroner's Court and you will be questioned on your actions by the coroner."

The police officers left the station and I was left wondering what was going to happen at Coroner's Court. Although I am not a worrier, I had never been to Coroner's Court or any court in my life. Everybody reassured me that all would be OK. It was then 0735 hrs and almost time to go home.

When it was my turn to attend the court case, I was seated quietly. Ray had also been summoned to appear in order to give evidence and also three firemen. We were all in uniform and we all sat together.

"All Stand," and everybody stood up as the coroner took his seat. The room was full and the CPR Lady kept glaring at me. Various people were called in turn by the coroner and were asked about the statements that they had made to the police a few days after the fatal accident. Then it was the CPR lady's turn.

She pointed repeatedly towards me while she was giving her evidence.

"I was keeping him alive," she said.

"How long did you do CPR for?" the coroner asked.

"About six or seven minutes, until he came and interrupted me," she said, pointing at me.

"And what are your qualifications?" he asked.

"I have a First Aid Certificate," she said.

"Was he alive until you were told to stop by the ambulance crew?"

"Yes, he was alive and moaning and it was not the crew who stopped me, it was him! He should be sacked," she said with anger rising in her voice.

"Thank you for your evidence," he said. "You are still under oath and you may be recalled. It is I who makes any recommendations, not you."

It was then my turn to be questioned.

"Please can you tell me briefly about the fatal accident. Start at the point when you arrived at the scene."

"As we arrived, I had to do a very rapid visual assessment of the scene. I saw a lady doing CPR on a trapped patient who appeared to have very severe injuries," I said. "I asked her to stop CPR so that I could do a proper check on the patient. She initially refused to let me do an assessment because she told me that she was keeping him alive. Within seconds, I told her to stop so that I could do a proper check for signs of life. I determined that all signs of life were absent. He had massive head injuries and he had a crushed chest."

"What are your qualifications to determine that?" he asked me.

"I hold a Miller Certificate issued by the National Health Service and also an Advanced Training Certificate issued by Cheshire County Ambulance Training School," I responded.

"So you are quite highly skilled?" he asked.

"Yes, sir."

There was a mumbling in the courtroom and people were still glaring at me. I was quite concerned as to what the outcome of the inquest would be.

"I am now calling Doctor Jacob," the coroner said.

A distinguished man in his fifties walked to the witness box and gave the oath on the Bible confirming that he would tell the truth.

"Please state your name and occupation."

"Doctor Thomas Jacob, Pathologist."

"Thank you, doctor, I will keep this short for you. I am sure that you are a busy man. Did you carry out the post mortem on anybody from this fatal accident?" he asked.

"Yes, I did. He was the male patient who had received CPR at the scene."

"Can you describe his injuries?"

The doctor went into great detail listing fractures to different bones of the skull, two bones in his left leg were broken, nine ribs and the breastbone were all broken. He also described some severe internal injuries. At that point, the coroner stopped the doctor.

"Can you describe the internal injuries for me?" he asked.

"I can list them. A lacerated liver, ruptured left kidney, punctured left lung, detached aorta."

"So these were significant injuries. Can you give a cause of death?" the coroner asked.

"Yes, he died from a detached aorta."

"What is a detached aorta and how does it affect the body?"

"A detached aorta is where the largest blood vessel in the body — the aorta — detaches or is ripped out of the heart."

"What causes that and what are the effects?"

"Usually a high-speed impact and the result is almost instantaneous death."

"Did you say almost instantaneous death? Could CPR keep him alive?"

"Death would be almost immediate, within seconds and no amount of CPR could have changed the situation," the doctor stated.

"Thank you, Doctor Jacob. You are free to leave."

Immediately after the doctor left, the coroner recalled the CPR lady to the witness box.

"Madam, you have heard expert testimony from Dr. Jacob that death would have been almost instantaneous. How dare you come into my court and lie about the ambulanceman and try to destroy his career?" She was as red as a beet root but she never spoke.

"You are lucky that I do not have you prosecuted for perjury," he continued. "You will now publicly apologise to Mr. Gillatt."

She almost spat out the muffled apology, and as if to humiliate her even more, the coroner claimed that he could not hear her and told her to repeat it louder.

I was then recalled and thanked for my work on that night, a night that I still remember vividly, even though almost 50 years have gone by since then. I remember being very relieved when the whole case was finally over and I had been exonerated of any blame.

I realized that I had come a long way in the last few years before that harrowing incident. The advanced training and the ability to keep gaining more and more experience was proving to be priceless. But there were still times when training could not solve everything and neither could experience. You just had to learn from things and move on. And fortunately, not all calls were RTAs and DOAs. Sometimes we were able to help save lives in other ways.

Which brings me to another kind of call that I also remember vividly and those were the times I had the opportunity to help a mother deliver a baby. I did quite a number of them over the years, where the little ones could not wait until we could get their Mom to the hospital.

One of the babies was born to the wife of Andy Murphy, one of our control officers. I was working with Stan Green and Andy came running into the Mess Room with an emergency call form. It was to his house and his wife was expecting her baby very soon.

We flew out the station as fast as we could, and when we arrived at the address, Andy's wife was lying in the hallway just inside the front door and she told us that the baby was on its way. We set about preparing to deliver the baby where she was and in no time at all, the baby arrived! It was a little boy and both mother and baby were fine.

After taking Mrs. Murphy to the Maternity Unit at the hospital, we cleaned up and replaced our maternity kit and blankets. Andy had followed us to the hospital and was thanking us for the job we had done. We used to see Liam occasionally at the ambulance station as he was growing up. He used to come with Andy, and while Andy washed his car, Liam would sit in the driver's seat in the ambulance. Twenty-one years after he was born, I was to see Liam again but then it was under completely different circumstances.

There was still a lot of life and learning on my plate before that fateful future day. One of the unusual days along the way, I still remember like it was yesterday. My Hospital Training started at 0800 hrs on one Monday morning at the Stockport Infirmary. Since I knew most of the staff and they knew me, it was fairly easy to fit in. I was given a white coat to wear and a notebook in order to make notes. I was there to learn and it felt like it was going to be a great week.

I was given an itinerary as to what I would be doing during the week. Two days in the Casualty Department, half a day in the plaster room (where plaster casts were applied to broken bones), half a day in X-ray and two days in the operating theatre. It was certainly going to be an exciting week.

As patients were brought in by ambulance, my job was to listen to the handover from the ambulance crew and decide where to put the patient. I was shadowed by a nurse who interrupted if I went wrong or kept quiet if I was doing OK. My ambulance colleagues were asking me about the Hospital Training program because they were all going to have to do it. I gave them the information and although mostly crews were keen to take it on, some others were nervous about it. I reassured them and told them to ask questions.

I thoroughly enjoyed my two days in the Casualty Department and on the second day, I was shadowing a Dr. Singh. I had been warned by the nurses that this new doctor, whom I had never met before, used hypnosis extensively as part of his treatment especially for dislocations. I was told not to look at him because he could instantly hypnotise people. Wow, that was scary but he promised not to hypnotise me since I was his *assistant* for the day.

When a patient with a dislocated elbow was brought in, Dr. Singh examined the patient and then asked me to examine him. I was not sure why but he sent the man for x-ray. While the patient was away having his x-ray done, Dr. Singh asked me how I might treat the patient. I suggested either a local anaesthetic or a general anaesthetic.

"Not necessary," he said. "When he comes back to us, I want you to watch what I do."

No sooner had he said that than the patient was wheeled back into our department.

"How are you feeling?" he asked the patient.

"Bloody awful, please can I have something for the pain?"

Dr. Singh started to recheck the patient's pulse and the colour of the skin on his affected arm.

"Let me check your pupils, please," said the doctor.

I thought that this must be it. Will he hypnotise him now?

Dr. Singh turned to me and said, "There you are, he feels no pain now. I will reduce the dislocation in a moment."

And that is exactly what he did, literally thirty seconds later the dislocation was reduced and a nurse was putting a supportive bandage around the elbow.

"As soon as the nurse finishes, I will wake him up," the doctor said.

Turning to the patient, he said: "When I get to one, you will wake up and you will feel fine. Four, three, two, one."

The patient opened his eyes and was instantly awake and smiling.

"How is your elbow?" asked Dr. Singh.

"Not too bad thanks," said the patient. And with that he hopped off the trolley and went to make his follow up appointment at the reception desk.

That was just one of many surprising things that I saw and learned while taking training at the hospitals in the area and through the Training School. It all added up to an incredible bank of knowledge and experience, for which I continue to be eternally grateful. But still not every day was easy and not every co-worker was as open as I was to all the new techniques and procedures, not to mention the many characters that we came in contact with.

But to me, it was a joy, a great career path, and I got a great deal of satisfaction from my work. I always wondered what was coming next and sometimes, the answer was something I could never have foreseen.

10. Nobody Likes Change

As April 1974 was approaching, the Ambulance Services in Great Britain were going to be affected by boundary changes to most of the counties in the country. These changes would take place on April 1st 1974. The part of Cheshire where I worked was going to be absorbed into a new metropolitan service and they were calling the new entity the Greater Manchester Ambulance Service. There were very little change for us but Manchester was going to undergo huge changes, mainly with regards to the areas that would be covered and in the training that would be coming up for them.

The transition took about twelve months to establish in order to get all the crews working the same way, using similar radios and radio procedures for example. The colour system was removed from radio communications, and there were also changes to Control Rooms, uniforms, vehicle maintenance facilities and a whole host of other things. And in the midst of all this, the daily work continued unabated, only now we were being sent to areas that most crews did not know. I had the advantage of knowing most of Manchester like the back of my hand since I was born there, grew up there and I had worked there up until five years before the time of the major changes.

I found that actually we were mainly kept busy in our own area with just the occasional job in the "new" area. And I had been back to the Training School for a two-week refresher course and I had been welcomed back like a long lost relative by Mr. Andrews. I enjoyed the refresher and I got to see some even newer procedures and equipment. As always, I thoroughly enjoyed the training.

Back on duty again on day shift with Stan, we had done the usual routine of checking equipment and replenishing supplies as necessary. Then at 1000 hrs, the firemen started doing some drills and practicing extrication techniques from wrecked vehicles. They always had a couple of scrap cars available with which to practice. Stan and I went to watch them and pretty soon we were roped in to help. We were bombarded with questions about how to deal with certain injuries and how to get injured people off a high ledge or a roof. We discussed how they could utilize some of their equipment so that injuries were not aggravated. I think we would have continued working with all that but suddenly we got the bells. I ran for the ticket and down again to the ambulance.

"House fire, persons reported, Stan, Parsonage Avenue, Bramhall."

"Quebec 1, red to Bramhall, over."

"Roger Quebec 1, 1020, we have had five calls for this and the Fire Brigade say it is a working job." This meant that it was a real fire.

"Quebec 1, roger, over."

"Base out."

That address was right at the far boundary of our area and luckily the traffic was light since it was after rush hour. Stan was driving like a man possessed weaving in and out of traffic at an incredible speed.

At 1032 hrs, we approached the avenue where the fire was. As we turned into the avenue, Stan braked hard and stopped. This was a cul-de-sac and Stan was leaving room for the fire brigade.

"Quebec 1, red at scene, this is a bad one, a bad fire, over."

"Roger, 1032, base out."

There were dozens of people at the end of the cul-de-sac all shouting and screaming at us to do something. Flames were shooting out like a blow torch from every window and the front door. The flames were shooting out of the downstairs windows a distance of eight to ten feet. It was a roaring inferno. We were told that there were children in the house and we made a number of attempts to get near but the heat was unbelievable. I had not experienced such a fire since the time when I was a volunteer fireman some years before.

Within a couple of minutes, the fire brigade arrived and eight firemen in breathing apparatus (BA) and dragging fully charged hoses started to fight their way in. The fire would not go down to start with and other men started hosing the house from the outside. I was about to call our Control Room with a situation report when there was a shout from the garden of the burning house.

Some firemen had forced their way in and brought out a small body.

The body was blackened and charred beyond recognition as a child. Instead, it looked like a small log and it was steaming from the heat in its body and the water from the hoses. Oh, no, I thought this is a nightmare for the family and for the firemen and for us.

I ran back to the ambulance for some blankets to cover the body with and by the time I returned, there was a second body in the same condition laid out on the lawn. Although the house was still smouldering, the actual fire was nearly out. The house was gutted, only the four brick walls and some of the roof remained.

It was impossible to get our ambulance any nearer since there were six fire engines in the avenue and hoses laid out like demented snakes. We decided that once the crowds had been moved by the police, we would recruit some help to carry the two bodies to the ambulance.

Stan went to turn the ambulance around and reverse it as near as he could. We were still about thirty yards away from the bodies. In no time at all, the avenue was cleared and with the help of the firemen, we placed the two bodies onto the stretcher trolleys. The bodies were still steaming and of course, they had that unique smell of burnt and chard flesh — a smell that once you have smelled it, you can *recall* the smell vividly even years later.

As we closed the backdoor, a fireman came over to us in a dreadful state. This was his first fatal fire and he had been part of a two-man BA team who had found the first child. He was distraught and we tried to comfort him but he was inconsolable. We told him that he needed to talk to his colleagues about this fire when he got back to station.

There was no other help for any of us in those days. Therapy and mental health issues were not common things to talk about. It is a wonder we did not end up in psychiatric care although some of us would need help years later. As the young fireman walked away, a shout went up again for more blankets because another body had been found. This time it was a tot, probably about two or three, and like the other two, this body was also burnt beyond recognition and it too was steaming. It was a most frightful sight to see and a sight that never quite leaves you.

Our ambulance was then full of charred children, three in total. Their ages were difficult to work out but I think one was about seven, one about five, and the smallest probably only a toddler.

The fire brigade had finished searching the house and confirmed that there was nobody else in the house. We were ready to take our wretched load to be certified.

"Quebec 1 to base, over."

"Base, Quebec 1, over."

"Quebec 1 to base, red to Stockport, three children, all Code 1s, over."

"Base, roger Quebec 1, 1113, base out."

And there followed the routine for certification at the hospital and then over to the mortuary. It was so very, very hard to carry those little children into the mortuary but we did so reverently and gently laid them onto the stainless steel tables. They looked like they had been sacrificed for some ritual that nobody knew about. It was one of the saddest days that I have ever had. I can still see the charred bodies even now. It was beyond comprehension. We were both in a state of shock and like all emergency service personnel, we had to subdue our emotional feelings and carry on as normal.

"Quebec 1 to base, over."

"Base, Quebec 1, over."

"Quebec 1, green at the mortuary, over."

"Roger Quebec 1, return to station, 1150, base out."

We travelled back to station in silence. We were both lost in our own thoughts and feelings. I wondered how the young fireman on his first fatal fire had done. Had he talked to his colleagues, was he still at the scene, what would happen to him?

"Quebec 1 to base, over."

"Base, Quebec 1, over."

"Quebec 1, green on station, over."

"Roger, 1214, base out."

As you never know what will happen next, I happened to deliver my first set of twins that same day. We had finished our lunch and we sat down in the TV room to watch the lunchtime news which was regretfully all the usual doom and gloom.

At 1328 hrs, we received a call which although not a 999 call, it was a call with some priority. It was to an address in an area called Gatley which was about three miles away. As we were making our way there without the two-tones or flashing blue lights, the radio burst into life,

"Base, Quebec 1, over."

"Quebec 1, go ahead, over."

"Quebec 1, this is now an emergency call, the birth is imminent, 1339, over."

"Quebec 1, roger, two minutes away, over."

As we pulled up at the address, a lady met us and said that the baby was about to be born. Stan grabbed the Maternity Pack and followed me into the house and up the stairs to a bedroom. A lady was lying on the bed and she was shouting in pain.

"Hello, we are the ambulancemen. I don't think we are going to get you to the hospital, are we? I'm just going to examine you and then we will make a decision. How often are your contractions?"

Before she could answer another strong contraction started.

"That was less than two minutes. OK. When is your baby due?" I asked politely.

"Last Tuesday and it's two."

"What do you mean it's two?" I asked, kind of startled.

Just then another contraction came, and the baby's head was crowning. This was going to be a delivery in the house. Stan went down to the ambulance and informed Control of our situation and requested a midwife to attend.

By the time Stan was back, the baby was delivered, wrapped in a blanket and placed next to the mother who was now telling me that she was expecting twins! *Bloody hell, I thought what do we do now?*

"Stan, can you get the other maternity pack? There's another on its way!"

By the time the midwife arrived, we had two bouncing baby boys and mother and babies were doing fine.

"We done lads, you will be after my job next," she joked.

"No thanks, we love our job too much," I said with a smile. "Although it is nice to bring new life into the world occasionally."

Soon we had the patient and the two babies in the back of the ambulance and we were on our way to Wythenshawe Maternity Hospital about five miles away.

"Quebec 1, base, over."

"Base, Quebec 1, over."

"Quebec 1 mobile to Wythenshawe Mat., mother and twins on board, over."

"Roger Quebec 1, well done, 1436, base out."

I chatted with the midwife and the patient and I thought what a great way the day had turned out.

"Quebec 1 to base, arrived at Wythenshawe, over."

"Roger, Quebec 1, 1445, base out."

"Quebec 1, clear at Wythenshawe, over."

"Roger Quebec 1, return to station, 1512, over."

"Quebec 1 roger."

The rest of the shift was quiet and we were really glad about that. We felt that we'd had more than enough excitement for one day.

The job continued with its highs and lows and day by day, I continued to gain a huge amount of experience. Over the next few years, I gained a number of professional qualifications by going to college in the evenings when shifts allowed and by studying at home and at work when I was on night shift.

By 1976, I was promoted to the position of Leading Ambulanceman (L/A) and that gave me some wider scope for various improvements at the local level. Some of the advantages of promotion were that I would have one regular workmate all the time and we could develop a standard way of how we worked.

My permanent mate was to be Stan Green. Stan had been one of my two partners for a number of years. I liked the new change and it turned out that we could read each other after a while, that each look or facial expression to each other was instantly understood which made us quick on the job and very efficient.

The promotion also meant a change in the shift pattern. It was now a pattern of twelve-hour day shifts one week followed by twelve-hour night shifts the next week. That system was perpetual. Around the same time, the Control Room, which had always been part of the station itself, was closed down and moved to a newer facility in Manchester. All calls were then being sent by direct line telephone.

If you asked me, I would have said this was a step backwards because then we had to answer the phone and actually write the details down, which delayed our turn out time slightly. But we had to get used to the system because it was supposed to *improve efficiency.*

The L/As like me were also given a brand new ambulance, much bigger and faster than the old ones. It had lots of new equipment some of which was built in such as oxygen outlets, and a suction unit for suctioning out blood, mucus, and vomit from the throat and upper airway.

A radio handset had been fitted in the rear of the ambulance for the attendant to use in order to pass information to the Control Room about a patient. Crews were not controlled by hospitals and everybody made their own decisions regarding treatment, just as long as they were qualified to give the treatment that they chose. The ambulance also had two trolleys which were locked against the walls but when released they could be raised up in height and adjusted to multiple posture settings. They were a big advance.

Stan and I were on days and although the day shift was not usually particularly busy, we were kept on the move for most of the day. One day, we were having our evening meal at about 1900 hrs when suddenly the phone rang.

"Cheadle Hulme." That was how we answered the phone then, not hello, but just the station name.

"Emergency for you. Child injured on grass land, Jepson Avenue, Cheadle Hulme. No other details. 1905."

"On the way, thanks."

"Come on Stan, emergency on Jepson Avenue, a child injured," I said.

"Quebec 1, mobile, over."

"Roger, 1907, base out."

Stan liked to drive and I was happy with that. Being the attendant all the time gave me vastly more experience treating patients since I basically became the permanent medic in the back of the ambulance.

Jepson Avenue was about five hundred yards from the station and as Stan drove in that direction, we spotted a man waving frantically at the bottom of the avenue.

"Quebec 1, at scene, over."

"Roger, 1909, base out."

I jumped out while Stan opened the doors and dropped the steps. I asked the man what the problem was.

"Over there, see that dummy hanging in the tree?" he said frantically. "I think it is a child. There were a gang of kids playing cowboys and Indians. I am sure it is a child."

The tree was about fifty yards away so Stan and I ran towards the tree and as we got there, it was obvious that there was a child hanging by the neck in the tree about ten feet off the ground.

"Bloody hell," Stan muttered quickly. "If I lift you up, can you grab that branch and get up there?"

In a second Stan had lifted me enough to get to the branch that the child was hanging from. He was purple in the face and not moving. As I tried to release the loop of rope around the boy's neck, I realised that I would have to cut it. I balanced myself a bit, and with my legs curled around the branch, I took out my knife and just as I was about to cut the rope, I realised that the child would drop to the ground.

I was about to ask Stan to get a ladder when a neighbour came sprinting to us with a step ladder. The boy was about eight, so he would not be too heavy and once the ladder was placed against the tree, Stan leapt up and took the child's weight. I cut the rope and the boy was free. I managed to get a foot onto the ladder and in a heartbeat, I was down as well.

Stan was running to the ambulance carrying the boy, and I was chasing behind. I was shouting to the few people that were there if anybody knew the boy and to my amazement, Stan said that he knew him.

I had secured the child's airway with an OPA, had him on oxygen and since he was not breathing, I had started CPR. I had to kneel on the stretcher trolley in order to maintain constant CPR.

"OK Stan. Go like hell to Stockport, inform Control to let the Casualty Department know what we are bringing in," I said quickly and kept on with the CPR compressions.

"Quebec 1 to base, over."

"Base, Quebec 1, over."

"Quebec 1 leaving scene for Stockport, please let them know that we have an eight or nine-year-old boy in cardiac arrest from being hung, CPR in progress, ETA is ten minutes, over."

"Roger Quebec 1, 1920, over."

I continued the CPR and Stan drove very fast to Stockport. I could see that the child's colour improved somewhat but he was still not breathing. I continued uninterrupted CPR and as I glanced out of the darkened side window, I saw that we had arrived at the hospital. As Stan open the doors, a doctor and nurse jumped in to do a check of the boy. The doctor told me to stop CPR for a moment and then suddenly declared, "There is a faint heartbeat, get him into resus immediately."

We unloaded the trolley and dashed into the resuscitation room with the boy. As we were about to lift him onto a hospital trolley, the doctor wanted to put in an IV drip and intubate him. I watched as the intubation tube was passed through the vocal cords and down into the windpipe in order to secure the airway from blockages. I wished at that time that we had been trained in that procedure but that was to come in the future.

We were both given some high praise from the doctor after I did the handover and briefly told him the story. The doctor asked if we could arrange for him to go out on calls with a crew, not to interfere but to see how we manage to do our job in a moving vehicle. He was astounded that I had managed to do effective CPR while being driven at high speed and with the siren blaring and still it had been successful. We told the doctor that we would try and arrange something during the next few weeks.

Stan and I cleaned up and tidied the back of the ambulance.

"Quebec 1 to base, over."

"Base, Quebec 1, over."

"Quebec 1, clear at Stockport Infirmary, over."

"Quebec 1, what was your arrival time at Stockport, you failed to call, over."

"Quebec 1, 1928, we were busy saving a life, over."

"Roger Quebec 1, return to station, 2017, over."

Stan was very quiet, but he told me that he knew the boy and his family.

"You did an unbelievable job resuscitating him. Let's hope he survives," said Stan.

I thanked Stan for his compliment and agreed that survival would mean everything.

"Quebec 1 to base, over."

"Base, Quebec 1, over"

"Quebec 1, on station, over."

"Base out."

The boy did survive and I spent the next fifteen years watching him walk past the ambulance station with a severe limp in his leg. Stan told me that he also had a slight speech impediment, but the main objective had been accomplished on that terrible night, and he had survived. In a job where we don't always hear the outcome, I was proud of our success and

I knew it was only because of our training and experience that we were able to make such a difference. Still there were more advances to come, some that I could not have even imagined in the mid to late 1970s, and I couldn't wait to learn them all.

11. Life-Saving Equipment and Specialised Skills

By the early 1980s, there was a lot of talk in the ambulance service about a new mobile piece of equipment called a Defibrillator. A defib, as it became known, was a piece of equipment that was used in cases of cardiac arrest and may terminate the chaotic activity in the heart which had caused the heart to stop. Its action was like pressing the reset button on a piece of electrical equipment or pressing *control, alt, delete* on your keyboard.

The defibrillators were very expensive in the beginning, around £10.000 or about $18,000 in Canadian terms. And that was without any training. Fortunately, two things happened which would transform training even further than it had already come. There was an Emergency Department Consultant at a local hospital that was an advocate of *advanced care* by ambulance crews and he had offered to train a small group in defibrillation, intubation, IV access and blood pressure monitoring and interpretation. He would do all this in his own time provided that the group that he chose to train would give a 100% commitment to the training.

We were excited at the prospect of the training, and ready to give it our 100%, but the only problem was that we did not have any of the equipment that was needed. Nonetheless, we pushed forward and the group was chosen and I was happy to be in that group. It was decided that we would raise funds for the equipment by doing car boot sales (yard sales) and also by persuading companies to donate cash.

It ended up taking almost a year but between the three stations in the area, we finally had enough money to buy our own defibs and equip one ambulance at each station. They were American-made manual machines, the kind where the attendant made the decision to deliver the shock or not and the machine itself weighed about twenty-five pounds. These were much heavier than the first aid type ones of today that weigh only about four or five pounds.

Training was intense and involved learning a large number of cardiac rhythms, practicing setting up drips and inserting the cannula into each other's veins. We had to each complete thirty supervised intubations on real patients in an operating department which was no small task. We had to ask to be invited to various hospitals in order to achieve those thirty intubations. Each intubation had to be completed within between fifteen and twenty seconds.

It took almost a year to complete the full training and pass the exam which was a six-hour practical and written exam. I passed the exam and I became a *paramedic* with all the skills and tools which went with the title. I was elated and I could not help feeling that my comments over all the years of *not enough training* for the job were finally justified.

Soon after qualification and receiving most of my equipment, I was informed that we were changing to a newer defibrillator. The newer one was a S&W 600 and it was a much more modern machine and also manual, still not automated. With this machine, the operator would read the cardiac action on a screen and then make the decision to defibrillate or not.

We received our S&W 600 and although Stan and I were off-duty prior to our night shift, I got a phone call at home telling me that the new machine was installed in our ambulance. I was one of two leading paramedics who were allowed to touch it!

I came into work the following evening and when I was in the back of the ambulance checking over the new defib equipment and all the other equipment, Stan joined me.

"Ah, I see that you have your *new toy*," he said. "Does it work?"

"I was waiting for you so that you can see how we test it."

"OK, thanks," he said.

I showed Stan how to test that it was working. We then checked the accessories that were in a pouch attached to it which included the electrode gel which was actually a well-known brand of lubricant called K-Y Jelly. The jelly had to go onto the metal paddles before pressing them onto a patient's chest because without the lubricant, you would likely only get an unreliable reading of the activity of the heart. The jelly also creates a good skin contact and prevents burning of the skin.

Finally, everything was checked including our fluids for infusion and the Intubation Kit.

"Let's have a coffee, Stan."

"Good idea while we can."

Because there were very few paramedics at that time, the Control Room tended to send paramedic crews to incidents that were miles away. It never occurred to them that the delay in a paramedic crew getting to a far-off scene was wasting valuable patient care time when other crews were much nearer.

At around 2100 hrs, the phone rang.

"Cheadle Hulme."

Stan had answered the phone and was writing down the job: "Urgent admission, an Unstable Angina (a heart condition), Dr. Gee is at the house."

This was not a lights and siren job but there was considerable urgency particularly with the doctor still at the house. Stan drove us at a nice pace to the address about four miles away in Bramhall and pulled up outside the home.

"Quebec 1 to base, at location, Bramhall, over."

"Roger Quebec 1, 2124, base out."

Doctor Gee met us as we got out of the ambulance.

"Hi Ron. Hi Stan," Doctor Gee said. He knew us and we knew him very well. In fact, we called each other by our first names.

"Hello John, what have you got for us?" I asked.

"He is forty-two years old and a very independent man who refuses to listen to me. He has unstable angina and I have arranged for his admission to Stepping Hill hospital."

"Go and see if you can talk some sense into him, Stan. You're bigger than Ron," he said with a chuckle.

Stan went to talk to the man and explained that we would put him on our carry chair and bring him out to the ambulance to save him walking.

"You can bugger off with your chair. I will walk," the patient said.

Stan pleaded with him but he was adamant that he was walking. After a few minutes, the patient, whose name was Mr. Frank White, came walking slowly out of the house and his concerned wife told us that she would follow us in the car. As Mr. White got into the ambulance, I told him that he must lie down on the trolley.

"I'm not lying on a bloody narrow bed like that, I'll fall off."

"No, you won't," I assured him. "I will strap you on, like having a seat belt on but lying down."

"I don't care, I am sitting up."

"Mr. White, we will be in serious trouble if we take you into the hospital and you are not lying down. How would it be if I raise your head and shoulders up a little?"

"Oh, OK, I don't want to get you lads into trouble," and with that he was on the trolley, strapped in and we were ready for the off.

"Quebec 1 to base, over."

"Base, Quebec 1, over."

"Quebec 1, leaving Bramhall for Stepping Hill Hospital, over."

"Roger Quebec 1, 2145, base out."

Stan drove very steadily and made sure that he missed all the potholes on the roads. We had only been going for a few minutes and I had taken my eyes off Mr. White for a split second and as I looked back at him, he was changing colour and becoming purple in the neck and face. I shook him but got no response. He had arrested which meant his heart had stopped.

"Stan, pull up. He's arrested," I said loudly.

"You shouldn't joke about things like that," Stan said.

"Stan, stop now," I insisted.

Stan hit the brakes and stopped. In a split second, Stan had come from the cab into the back and saw that Mr. White had, in fact, arrested. Stan started CPR immediately as I was busy getting the Defib switched on and listening for a heartbeat through my stethoscope. I confirmed that he had arrested and I prepared to do a *paddle look*. That was where the metal pads were pressed onto the chest in order to register any movement in the heart. I jelled up the paddles and pressed them onto his chest.

His heart was in *fine ventricular fibrillation* (VF) and that was a rhythm that could very well respond to defibrillation. I adjusted the energy setting on the defibrillator and prepared to shock.

"VF Stan, I'm going to shock, stay clear."

I pressed the charging button and then the shock button. The patient twitched. Shock 1 delivered.

"Another paddle look, Stan, still VF, preparing to shock again, stay clear," I told Stan.

"Shocking now, stay clear." Still the same rhythm. The K-Y on the paddles was drying out, I needed some more.

"Stan, just put some more K-Y on the paddles for me," I asked.

As Stan went to pick up the tube it fell down the side of the trolley and he could not get to it.

"Oh, Bloody Hell, Stan! The paddles are drying." In a split second, I remembered that K-Y is water soluble so I spat on both paddles and gave them a rub together. It was enough to get the lubrication working again.

"Shocking now, stay clear." Buttons pressed and then another paddle look.

"We've got a rhythm, Stan," I said excitedly. "It's a sinus rhythm, a normal heartbeat. Just give it a minute and I will get some monitoring leads on him. Please could you get me the IV Kit?" I wanted to set up Intra Venous access to a vein so I could administer a drip.

Between us, we attached the monitoring leads to Mr. White's chest and while Stan helped me to find a vein by squeezing the arm, I prepared to cannulate a vein in Mr. White's arm. Cannulation is where a large bore needle is passed into a vein and then a drip is attached to it.

After a couple of minutes, Mr. White had settled down, but he was still unresponsive. All this activity had only taken less than ten minutes, but it seemed like hours. Stan went to tell Mrs. White that we had just had a minor hiccough with her husband and that we were going to a different hospital.

"Quebec 1 to base, over."

"Base, Quebec 1, over."

"Quebec 1, we are going directly to Stockport Infirmary, our patient arrested but he is breathing again after defibrillation, over."

"Roger Quebec 1, did you say after defibrillation, over."

"Quebec 1, Roger, a successful defibrillation, over."

After a short silence the Control Room answered back.

"Well done Quebec 1, shall we inform Stockport, over?"

"Quebec 1, Roger, over."

"Roger Quebec 1, 2200 hrs, base out."

Stan drove at a nice steady speed to Stockport and as he reversed up to the doors, a doctor and three nurses came out to meet us.

"Quebec 1 to base, arriving at Stockport, over."

"Roger Quebec 1, 2212, base out."

"Is this the cardiac arrest?" I heard a nurse ask.

"It was — but not now," I said.

Stan opened the doors and we started to lift the trolley out of the ambulance. As we placed the trolley on the ground and were just preparing to elevate it, Mr. White opened his eyes and spoke. As he looked at me he said, "Looking at you, I did not think that you could swear like that." I was dumbfounded, how could he know that I had sworn in the ambulance, he must be delirious.

"How are you feeling now, Mr. White?" the doctor asked.

"Better now but your colleague hurt my ribs when he was doing that pressing on my chest."

"How do you know what we were doing, you were unresponsive?" I asked him.

"I was watching everything that you did," the patient assured us. "I saw your mate drop that equipment down the side of the stretcher and I heard you swear."

By now the hair on the back of my neck started to stand up. He could not possibly have known anything about what went on. *He was dead.*

"I watched and heard everything. I was sitting up on top of your search-light," Mr. White insisted. "Then suddenly I was no longer there and I saw the lights getting brighter."

In the ambulance we had a large lamp that was fixed just inside the back doors. It was on a bracket which allowed us to swing it out to light up a small area if we were working in the dark outside.

"That must have been an *out of body experience*," I said to Stan. To have all your actions recounted by a dead man was a very strange feeling. That was the first time that I had encountered such an event but it wasn't the last.

As we transferred him onto the hospital trolley in the resus, I gave the doctor the paper trace from the defibrillator which clearly showed that he had been in arrest. The doctor was astounded that not only had we successfully defibrillated him, attached monitoring leads, and taken blood pressure readings but we also had a drip running.

"Who did all this?" asked the doctor.

"We did, between us," I explained.

"Who trained you to do all this and where did you get the defibrillator and IV equipment?" the doctor asked seeming to be amazed about it all.

I told him the story of our training and that we had bought our own defibrillator and other equipment.

"I have never heard of this being done before by paramedics," the doctor said. "Is this training going to be for everybody?"

"No, not at the moment, just a few crews in this area," I explained. "This is not the first successful defibrillation in this area. I think that there have been two others."

"Very well done, really, you have saved this man's life."

As Stan and I tidied the back of the ambulance, we were both almost overcome with an unbelievable feeling of gratitude for what we had achieved. It made me think back to when there was so much resistance to change and when a basic first aid certificate was *the* complete qualification needed. We had come a very long way and I knew we would continue to improve with even more ongoing training and more experience. I could foresee a time when all modern cities and towns would have this same level of paramedics on call whenever needed and they would have fully-kitted out ambulances, even more high tech than ours at that time. But we were chuffed to be on the leading edge of that new world.

"Quebec 1 to base, over."

"Base, Quebec 1, over."

"Quebec 1, clear at Stockport, over."

"Roger Quebec 1, how is your patient, over?"

"Quebec 1, he is doing well and joking with the nurses, over."

"That is a fine job you both did, return to station, 2242, over."

"Quebec 1 roger, over."

"Base out."

The rest of our night shifts had the usual mixture of calls including a few cardiac arrests where, unfortunately, we had been called too late. Also we responded to quite a few alcohol related calls and we got calls to unresponsive diabetics. As part of our paramedic kit were certain drugs and the drug of choice for diabetics who were unresponsive and in a hypoglycaemic state (where their sugar levels were far too low) was to inject the patient with Glucagon. This was a fast-acting drug which released sugar substitutes which are stored in the liver. In no time at all, the patient could respond and come around almost back to normal. It saved many unresponsive diabetic individuals from waking up in hospital.

Back on day shift and we had been very quiet, only five minor emergencies all day. We decided to eat our evening meal early. I think that the boredom of the day had made us hungry. I made the coffee and as we sat at the Mess Room table having our meal, we chatted about how Mr. White was doing. Just then the phone rang.

"Cheadle Hulme," Stan said.

"Emergency at Tallon Drive Cheadle Hulme, no further details, 1712."

"OK, thanks, on the way."

Stan reported the call to me. It's Tallon Drive, Cheadle Hulme, a three-nines, no details."

"Quebec 1 mobile over."

"Roger Quebec 1, 1713, base out."

Tallon Drive was a cul-de-sac not far from the station. Stan turned into Tallon Drive and pulled up at the address. The front door was open but there was nobody to meet us.

"Quebec 1, at scene, over."

"Roger Quebec 1, 1718, base out."

"I'll go up to the end and turn round," said Stan.

I jumped out and knocked on the front door. I shouted but no reply so I decided to walk into the house while continuing to shout, "Hello, Ambulance" but still no reply.

I looked into a room and there was nobody in there. As I got to the next room, there was a distinct smell of cooking. As I looked into that room, there were two untouched meals set out on the table. As I went closer to the table, it was obvious that the meals had only recently been served. I could see there was some steam coming off them.

I was about to leave the room when something dropped onto my head. Instinctively, I swept my hand over my hair and I looked up at the same time. My hand was covered in blood and the ceiling was splattered with blood and tissue. I looked around the room for the cause of this horrific mess and hidden behind some cushions was a child. It was difficult to estimate the age since his head had been smashed open.

I recoiled back instantly as I realised that this was a crime scene. As I was turning to leave the room, I spotted another child's foot sticking out from behind a couch. Oh no, I thought, not another, but it was. This child's head and face had been chopped to bits. I ran out to Stan and asked him to get the police there immediately.

I told Stan what I had found and he told me that I had blood on the side of my head and it had dried onto my ear. He got some sterile wipes and cleaned me up. I was in something of a daze and as we waited for the police, we decided to stay outside and not touch anything. Within a couple of minutes, the police arrived, and the Police Inspector asked me to show him where the children were. He insisted that I accompany him into the house for the purpose of continuity.

"Put your hands in your pockets and don't touch anything," he said.

I led the way into the dining room and just stood there while the images burnt themselves into my mind, never ever to be removed.

"Is this room exactly how you found it?" asked the police officer.

"Yes, it is."

"Did you touch anything?"

"When I had the blood drip onto my head, I looked around the room to see if I could find a source of the blood and bits of skull and brain that had also fallen. I moved that cushion to where you see it now."

"Was the body hidden by the cushion?" he asked.

"Yes."

"Did you touch anything else?"

"No, I left the room and went outside," I said, still feeling shaken.

"OK. Sorry to have made you come back into a scene like this, but as you found the children, you were needed for continuity of evidence. Give your statement to the constable outside and then you are free to go."

It was a most horrific site, one that I have never been able to forget.

After I had given a statement to the police, we were released since it was a murder scene.

"Quebec 1 to base over."

"Base, Quebec 1, over."

"Quebec 1, clear Tallon Drive, we have been released by the police, over."

"Roger Quebec 1, return to station, 1840."

"Quebec 1 roger."

"Base out."

Some weeks later, I learned that the children were hacked to death with a large meat cleaver and a suspect in the murders, a family member, had been arrested and charged.

For the first time in my career, I had started to feel that my *emotional repository* was getting full to overflowing with all the unspeakable sights that my colleagues and I were faced with on a regular basis. Those emotions and the horrific memories did not however overflow or show up again, until many, many years later, decades later. At the time, I just think that we became numb to these sights and sounds, the screams, the sobbing and the tortured facial expressions of our patients and their relatives. We tried to comfort them as best we could, but unfortunately nobody comforted us.

But there were other times as well, that were brighter and sometimes we created our own fun with pranks and jokes and stories. I always found that Sunday was a nice day to work on day shift for example. Someone was always nominated as the cook for the day and we always had a "Sunday Dinner" of some sort. A nice roast of meat, roasted potatoes and vegetables. It was like being at home. Occasionally the Control Room would try and use a different station if an urgent job came in but if it was an emergency, it was ours. Sunday was also cleaning day when an ambulance was stripped completely and cleaned inside from top to bottom.

I remember one Sunday that Stan was cooking and his speciality was pot roast. It was not my favourite, but it was well cooked and presented. We used a disposable sheet as a tablecloth and when dinner was ready, we called Control to see if we could stand down for our meal.

"No problem, Ron. Get your meal but if a three-nines comes in, you know it's yours?"

"Thanks very much, yes, just give us fifteen minutes and we will be done."

"OK. It's 1215 hrs as near as makes no difference."

So we started our meal which was actually really tasty. Stan had even gone to the trouble of doing some stewed rhubarb and custard for pudding.

At 1231, the bloody phone rang.

"Cheadle Hulme."

"Sorry about this, RTA on Stanley Road, Cheadle Hulme 1231."

"OK, thanks we are on the way."

Stan was just coming out of the kitchen and asked if it was an emergency.

"RTA, Stanley Road at the A34 end." Stanley Road was a long road so we would go into it at the start. It was a narrow road, just wide enough for two vehicles and it had a few blind bends.

"Quebec 1 to base, mobile to RTA, over."

"Roger Quebec 1, 1232, base out."

It was about three miles to the location and as we turned into Stanley Road, we were immediately behind a line of stationary traffic. Nothing was coming the opposite way so we had an idea that this could be a bad one. As Stan cautiously drove past the long line of cars and into a severe blind bend, and we were at the scene.

"Quebec 1 at scene, over."

"Roger Quebec 1, 1240, base out."

We both jumped out and we were met with a car which had driven under the back of a parked articulated lorry (a tractor trailer). The car was most of the way underneath the rear of the trailer but there was no sound coming from the car.

"You're smaller than me. Can you wriggle in under the trailer?" said Stan.

I started to get underneath and as I got further under, I could see through the twisted metal what looked like a person's back.

"Stan, call for the fire brigade, persons' trapped," I shouted.

"Will do. Are you OK under there?" he asked.

"I'm OK, Stan."

As I got further in and peered into what was left of the rear part of the car, a sight of unspeakable horror met me. The driver had been decapitated at shoulder level and his right shoulder, neck and his pulverised head were lying on the back seat.

Almost at the same time, I saw what I thought was a child in the back of the car under the twisted metal. I tried to reach in to check the child, but I could not reach. As I came out from under the wreck, Stan asked me again: "Are you OK, you look bloody pale?"

"We have a decapitation — at the shoulders," I said quietly. "Worst still, there's a kid in there that I can't get to."

"The fire brigade will be here in a few minutes, I can hear the sirens," Stan said, trying to sound as normal as he could. This was a bad, bad one, we both knew it.

Moments later *our* firemen arrived, and I quickly briefed them as to what I had discovered.

They did a quick assessment and then started to winch the car out as far as they could from underneath the trailer. They covered the driver's body and we were told the police would arrange for the removal after photographing every part of the scene. They winched the wrecked car out just enough for us to check the child.

As the fire brigade were cutting around the child in order to release him, I started to do some checks prior to setting a drip up. The child looked like he was dressed in boy's clothes. His skin was pale and cold and his pulse rate was very rapid.

"Stan, I think that this child has suffered internal injuries with severe internal bleeding," I reported. "Can you bring the oxygen?"

As the child was released, we were able to see that he did not have a mark on him except for bruising on the left side of his abdomen. But I still feared something was going on inside.

"Could be a spleen, what do you think, Stan?"

"Very likely," he said. "Are you putting the drip up?"

"No, it will take too long, but once he is in the ambulance, go like shit to Stockport."

The firemen were a huge help getting the child onto our trolley and into the ambulance, plus they helped us gather our equipment up quickly.

"Quebec 1 to base."

"Base, Quebec 1, over."

"Quebec 1, leaving Stanley Road for Stockport, a very fast run. Please inform them ETA nine minutes, eleven or twelve year old male, unresponsive with suspected severe internal bleeding."

"Roger Quebec 1, 1308, base out."

As Stan pulled away from the scene, a police traffic car pulled along-side the ambulance. The police officer shouted to Stan, "Where are you going?"

"Stockport Infirmary."

"I'll take you, just follow me."

We now had a police escort which was a terrific help but police cars still can go much faster than ambulances. As we approached a number of junctions controlled by traffic lights, they had police cars stop the traffic for us. It was fantastic organisation at such short notice.

Stan drove like I have never seen him drive before constantly giving me a running commentary about a left turn, a right turn, a roundabout, all in case I lost my balance.

I was working on the child the whole time, maintaining his airway, giving him oxygen and monitoring his levels of response which regretfully had not changed.

"Quebec 1, arrived Stockport, over."

"Roger, 1317, base out."

We unloaded our patient and rushed him into the resus where all the assembled staff pounced on the boy to begin their attempt to save his life.

Dealing with children is very hard on emergency service professionals. Unfortunately, sometimes it becomes just too much to handle. We stayed in the Casualty Department for some time assisting when asked. We also watched the staff desperately fighting to save the child's life. IVs were set up and it started to become apparent that the outcome would not be good.

We decided that we could not wait any longer and so we left. We tidied the ambulance and finally we were ready to call control.

"Quebec 1 to base, over."

"Base, Quebec 1, over."

"Quebec 1, clear at Stockport, over."

"Roger Quebec 1, return to station, 1401."

"Quebec 1 roger."

"Base out."

As we drove back to station, we chatted about the job and about how we could have done things differently or better. We decided that there was nothing else that we could or should have done differently. We had done our best. We just hoped that our best was good enough.

"Quebec 1 to base, over."

"Base, Quebec 1, over."

"Quebec 1, back on station, over."

"Roger, base out."

"We never had our rhubarb, do you want some now?" asked Stan.

"Yes, that would be nice and I'll make the coffee."

I was glad when our shift ended, and I could go home. The sight of the decapitated pulverised head and shoulders lying in the back of the car were constantly foremost in my mind. I felt pretty sure it would eventually go away, at least I hoped it would.

The following day, Stan and I were on days again and we found ourselves at Stockport Infirmary. We were chatting with some of the casualty staff when one of them told us that the child from yesterday had died. We half expected that news but we were hoping for the best. At that moment, the doctor who treated the boy told us that he thought that he died from a ruptured spleen. At least we knew what had killed him and in fact there was nothing that anybody could have done for him.

The rest of our shift was very quiet which we were really glad of.

Another day that we watched out for was Saturday. Saturday day shifts had a habit of being either very busy or very quiet, rarely somewhere in between. Today Stan asked me to drive since he had a sore knee but he would take over if I was needed to treat a patient at *paramedic level* as he put it. Stan was a *technician*, a very high standard of skill, but not as high as a *paramedic.*

I agreed and we checked the ambulance and as normal, we then made a coffee. It was 0840 hrs and our other crew had gone out on a routine job. We sat chatting about this and that and since it was a nice day, we decided to sit outside. We had been there for about half an hour when a crew from another station called in with some paperwork for the office.

As they pulled out of the station, the phone rang.

"Cheadle Hulme."

"A shooting, Polner Avenue, Cheadle. We will send the police, 0937."

"OK, on the way."

"Quebec 1, mobile to Polner Avenue."

I drove at quite a good speed wondering where on Polner Avenue this address was.

"I have a friend that lives on Polner Avenue, Stan, I just can't remember his number. His wife is a policewoman, I think. I have never met her."

"Maybe she will be at the job," said Stan.

"Quebec 1, arriving scene, no police here yet."

"Roger, 0942, we will give them another call, base out."

We were met by a woman screaming and begging us to get her children out of the house.

"He's got a gun. He's got a shotgun and he's got the children. Get them out before he kills them!"

"Where is he in the house?" I asked.

"He was upstairs," she said.

"OK, the police will be here soon. We need to wait for them."

"*I'm am the police*. I'm a policewoman with Manchester Police."

My heart skipped a beat as I thought that this cannot be Derek that is involved.

"What's his name," I asked.

"Derek, but he will not answer me," she said with the panic still in her voice. "You try and get my children out before he shoots them, please help us."

I said to Stan that I knew this man, her husband. "He is in a service club that I belong to. I think that we should try and talk to him while we wait for the police."

Stan nodded and as we approached the open front door, I shouted up to him.

"Derek, it's Ron from the club. Are you OK? Your wife has called us." No response.

"Where are the children, Derek?" I tried again.

There was still no answer and by now, we were slithering up the stairs slowly and silently along the treads and then the floor. The house was full of gunpowder fumes so obviously a gun had been fired. I knew that Derek had shotguns because I also had a shotgun and we both used to shoot together.

"Derek, which room are you in?"

No reply. By now, we were at the top of the stairs. I motioned to Stan with hand signals to check a bedroom to our left which by its decorating was a child's room. It was empty and Stan moved to the next room, also a child's room and it was empty too. At that same moment and still on our stomachs I entered the main bedroom.

I immediately stood up and shouted to Stan that I had found Derek. He was sitting up on the bed leaning against the headboard of the bed. He was dressed and he had a shotgun lying across his thigh. He had clearly placed the barrel of the gun in his mouth and pulled the trigger. Strangely, I could not take my eyes off his lower jaw and his teeth. That was all that was left of his head and face, and most of that was embedded in the wall and ceiling.

At this point, as horrific as this scene was, we had not yet found any children so we came back downstairs to look again. A police officer met us at the bottom. We turned around and took the officer up to Derek's body.

As we came back out of the house, a police officer approached us and told us that the children had actually gone to relatives the night before for the weekend and so had the dog. Derek's wife, in her distraught state, had forgotten that she had taken both the children and the dog to her Mother's for the weekend so that she and Derek could celebrate their wedding anniversary.

We were released by the police and as we left the scene, I began to think that when I go to Derek's funeral in a few days with all the other club members who were his friends, I would have a different picture of him in my mind compared to the way the others will remember him. The last time that you see somebody is the lasting picture that you have of them in your mind. That is why it is sometimes relatives are prevented from seeing a badly mutilated loved one because that could well become the lasting memory of their relative.

"Quebec 1 to base, over."

"Base, Quebec 1, over."

"Quebec 1, clear in Cheadle, suicide. The police will move the body later, over."

"Roger, Quebec 1, return to station, over."

"Quebec 1, roger, over."

"Base out."

On the way back to station, Stan asked me about the club that I belonged to and how long Derek had been a member. I had known Derek for about three years and although I must have met his wife at social functions, I didn't remember her. Fortunately, she did not recognise me while we were at the scene. I heard later that she never went back to work as a police officer and there was only the occasional mention of Derek at the club.

For those of us who deal with life and death every day, there often comes a time when you wonder if you can keep doing it, day in, day out. Especially when you see horrific scenes like the ones that are still burned into my memory from decades of this profession.

For Derek's wife, she gave up her career from what I could tell. Maybe she couldn't take the risk, being left as the only parent to her children, or maybe she couldn't live with the stress of being with the police force on the front lines every day. Everyone has their breaking point.

I couldn't help but wonder if I might ever reach a point like that. I loved my profession but when we went out to a *bad one,* you can't help but ask yourself the tough questions. For me, one of my very toughest *calls* ever was still to come.

RON GILLATT

THE GREEN MAN | TRUE STORIES OF A PARAMEDIC FROM THE ROADSIDE

12. A Night to Remember

Nights were always good shifts to work mainly because the roads were quieter, and we usually had some *proper jobs* to deal with. We also had some fun at night particularly playing tricks on each other. We were not always busy and not always dealing with really bad situations. The patient whom we had defibrillated some time ago, Mr. White, gave us an idea for playing a trick on one of our colleagues, John Strines, who frequently told us how frightened he was of ghosts.

Above the front door as you went into the station, there was a doorbell, the type with a domed bell and an arm which struck the dome when the button was pressed outside. So we decided to go into work early one evening and attach some very strong fishing line to the arm of the bell. We hid the fishing line around the banister on the staircase and the end of that line eventually reached to the side of an armchair in the TV room at the station. It was all ready for good natured tricks on our friend.

Once it was set, we all started work, did our checks on the ambulances and eventually settled down to watch TV until we were needed for a call. After about ten minutes, Philip Brown, who was sitting in the armchair, reached over the side that we could not see, and he gave the fishing line a tug.

John jumped up and we all looked at him in a pre-arranged way.

"What's wrong, John?"

"Somebody at the door. I'll go and see," John said as he headed downstairs.

"Bloody funny, there's nobody there," said John on his return.

After about five minutes, Philip discreetly reached down again and gave the fishing line another tug.

"There, did you hear that?" said John.

As per our game, I played along. "I didn't hear anything," I said. "Are you sure it rang?"

"Did nobody hear it ring?" said John.

"You must be imagining it or else it's a ghost," I said and we all turned back to the TV.

John looked panicked, unable to understand why no one else was hearing the bell ring and why no one was actually at the door. We let him believe it for quite a while, looking nervous and we pulled the trick a few more times before we couldn't keep up the charade and told him, with all the rest of us breaking up with good hearted laughter for the longest time. It was all in fun and it was a way that let off steam when things got a bit too tense. I think John forgave us but it was fun to see him worry and sweat about it.

Another game we played was similar and lots of fun. Our Chief Ambulance Officer would come to the station about every six weeks for an area meeting with the officers from the different stations in the areas around us. The chief always travelled with his Boxer dog which was pretty big and playful. Usually, particularly when it was warm, the CAO would leave the windows of his car half open so that his dog had fresh air.

There were two of us on the station who could do a very passable "dog bark" and so on the day the chief visited, we always hoped that we would be on station. Looking out of our Mess Room window, we were just to one side of the chief's car and we could see it parked at the front of the building. We would wait until the meeting had been in progress for about twenty minutes and all was quiet. The chief in his meeting and his dog asleep in the car.

We would then start *barking* as loud as we could, doing our best imitation. Almost instantly his dog would start barking loudly and bouncing around the interior of the car. Boxers seem to have very wet noses and of course the inside of the windows would be covered in mucus. The chief would hear the barking, excuse himself, come out to his car and reprimand the dog, before going back in.

We would let things settle down again and then off we would go again, *bark, bark* and *bark*. Same as before, out came the chief and reprimanded the dog. We would keep this up for an hour and the chief never knew why his dog always seem to have these bouts of hysterics when visiting at our station. It was pure comedy to watch the results of our little escapade.

Over the years, people who used to work at the station with us or in the

Control Room when we had one, they would stop by and call in to have a chat with us or perhaps wash their cars in the wash bay. It was fairly common for previous employees to bring their children or grandchildren in on a weekend to have a look at the ambulances and sit in the driving seat. It was fun for them when we would switch on the blue lights and sirens. I enjoyed those visits, seeing old friend and kids, and we got to watch many of their children grow up into adults.

One of the boys I really loved to see was Andy Murphy's son Liam. Andy would bring him to the station when I was working on weekends not only to see the ambulances but also because I had delivered him many years before. Andy used to say that I could watch him grow up. Eventually, Liam started to come to the station in his own car so that he could wash it and afterwards he would stay have a chat with us and share whatever was new. His father had been moved to the Control Room in Manchester years ago, but Liam still came in to see us. He had become quite a well-mannered young man and he had always called in to see Stan and me whenever we were on day shift on a Saturday or Sunday which occurred once a month.

One weekend we were working days on both Saturday and Sunday but those days we were very busy and we were in and out most of the time. We happened to be out on a call when Liam came to see us so we missed him. Never mind I thought, I will see him next time.

The Monday after our very busy weekend duty, I received a phone call at home and as a result I was asked to volunteer to join a civilian medical team being sent to treat people displaced by the Gulf War on the Iran-Iraq border just as that war was coming to an end. I was away as a volunteer with that medical team for a short time, which was an incredible experience, but that whole thing is perhaps for another book sometime.

But let me come back to this particular story here. When I returned from that placement, I was immediately back onto my normal shifts. Although it happened to be night shift on Saturday night and although I was back to my regular paramedic work, my mind was still on the trauma that I had seen and lived through on the Iran-Iraq placement. It turned out that our night at the station started out fairly quietly which I was glad about and we attended one minor emergency after which we were sent back to station.

Then at 2114 hrs, the phone rang.

"Cheadle Hulme."

"RTA, Polygon Road, Cheadle. Sounds like a bad one, 2114."

"OK, thanks, on the way."

"Come on Stan, sounds like a bad RTA, Polygon Road."

We ran down the stairs and out into the ambulance and off we went.

"Quebec 1, mobile over."

"Roger Quebec 1, 2115, base out."

The location, although slightly vague, would be easy to find since Polygon Road was not very long, maybe a mile at the most. As Stan turned onto Polygon Road under the railway bridge there was nothing in sight yet. But as the road undulated a little, we kept going. Suddenly we saw it, oh my God, what was all this debris on the road? Stan swerved to avoid hitting a vehicle battery directly in front of us and there were pieces of metal and glass everywhere.

"Quebec 1 at scene, this looks a real mess, will give you an update in a few minutes, over."

"Roger Quebec 1, 2120. I have another ambulance on stand-by in Stockport. Base out."

We were met by a most horrific sight: a twenty-seat small bus was in two pieces and a car was half-way through a stone wall. There were people lying in the roadway and some were still in what was left of the bus. It was difficult to comprehend where to start but start we had to and *quickly.*

I called to Stan to start to do a quick check of patients and figure out the priority of treatment — it's called triage. I started to check on my side of the wreckage and as I checked the first patient who was lying on the grass at the side of the road, I recoiled in shock as I saw the man's face. It was *our* Liam Murphy, the boy that I had brought into the world twenty-one years ago. *He was dead.* I could scarcely believe it was him. I had no time to mourn his horrible and sudden death or think about his poor parents who would be heartbroken. Instead, I took a deep breath and I forced myself to proceed with the triage process because that was my job. *Who could we save?*

As hard as it was, I had to leave him and move on to the next patient who, although still alive, was in fact critically injured. His chest was laid open and the blood loss was probably non-survivable. Suddenly Stan shouted that the two people in the car were dead but some people on or from the bus were in fact only suffering from minor injuries. I started to search the part of the bus that was nearest to me — both parts were about fifteen yards apart.

As I climbed into the wreckage, I found three people all unresponsive but alive and then another patient who was dead. Is this a nightmare that I am having or *is this really happening to me, I thought?*

"How many have you got that are injured, Stan?"

"I have eight who need hospital treatment."

"I have four. I am going to call control and see what help we can get."

The police were arriving in large numbers now and since the road was blocked, they closed both ends of the road.

"Quebec 1 to base, priority, over."

"Go ahead, Quebec1."

"Quebec 1, at Polygon Road, this incident is a multi-seat mini bus which has been hit by a car. The bus is in two separate pieces. We have four DOAs and twelve with multiple injuries. We need the fire brigade as two DOAs are trapped in a car. We also need seven or eight ambulances as quickly as possible, over."

"Roger Quebec 1, we will mobilise as many crews as we can find, but some may take some time to reach you, over."

"Roger, we are starting critical care treatment now so we will be on the portable radio on channel 1 if required, over."

"Roger, base out."

And with that, as we started our work, it became imperative that we did a thorough triage because we only had four bags of saline and a limited supply of other equipment. We worked hard establishing clear airways, some patients needed intubating, we set up IVs and generally focussed on trying to save lives as best as we could. It was not an easy task to do those procedures in the dark. Most streetlights were of the sodium type so they gave an orange glow and one that changes colours. Like for example the colour of the skin does not look the same under sodium lighting as it does under white light.

Nonetheless, I quickly established three IVs and intubated two patients when I heard the first sirens of a couple of approaching ambulances. Thank goodness, I thought, we desperately needed help there.

The first two crews started to ask which the priority patients were and fortunately, both of those ambulances had a paramedic as part of their crews. That was very important as some of the treatments that I had started could only be done and monitored by a paramedic. I briefed them on what we had done so far, and which was the order in which they should be taken to hospital.

The other crews agreed and the patient with the massive chest injuries was away first. I had intubated him and set up an IV. Just then three more crews arrived and again I briefed them on the order of evacuation from the scene. And so it continued for almost forty minutes until we were just left with the dead bodies.

The fire brigade had made it possible to lift the two bodies out of the car but, as it was subject to a criminal investigation, the police would not allow the bodies to be moved at that time. Apparently the car had been involved in a petrol station robbery some miles away and had been chased by the police. As the chase reached high speeds, the police did what they usually do in those cases and called off the chase about five minutes before the crash.

The other two bodies were photographed, where and how they were lying in relation to the wreckage and the police would move those bodies later. I told the senior police officer that Liam's dad was one of our officers and that we knew Liam very well.

"Bloody hell, what terrible luck for you lads coming and finding somebody that you know involved."

"I also delivered him when he was born," I said sadly, finally finding a moment to breathe and realize his loss.

"I don't know what to say. How we sleep at night I don't know," the police officer said. "But if you are like me, you only catnap."

With that the police officer gave me a hug. I had never seen an officer do that before but I think that he saw that, just at that moment, I needed it. I was on the very edge of breaking down.

"Not long ago, the husband of one of our policewomen committed suicide. He blew his head off with a shotgun. You should have seen the state that she was in, so I understand how you lads must feel."

"We did that job too and we saw how she was," said Stan. "She was in a terrible state."

The police officer just stared at Stan open-mouthed and did not say anything. He didn't need to, his face said it all.

A few days later, we found out that the bus that was cut in two was rented by Liam and his friends to take them into the city on a pub crawl, going to a number of pubs with the distinct probability of getting drunk. It was an event that was planned to celebrate Liam's twenty-first birthday.

A few other men from the station went to Liam's funeral and of course, I was there and so was Stan. Some of Liam's friends who had suffered minor injuries were there too. Some were bandaged up, but everybody wanted to be there. About ten people, Liam's friends and his family, got up and spoke about him.

Andy asked me if I wanted to say something, but I just could not. I was too emotional in such a moving setting. Andy spoke about Liam and how from an early age he loved coming to the ambulance station particularly when Ron and Stan were working. Andy also mentioned that I had delivered Liam when he was born and that Stan and I were the first crew at the scene that last night. Andy then turned to me and said how very sorry *he* was that I was the one to find Liam. He then thanked me for my friendship with Liam as he was growing up. This was a very, very hard funeral. Very hard. *I can't even express how hard.*

We did not see much of Andy after Liam's funeral. I think that the memory of bringing Liam to the ambulance station would have been too much for him. Then one morning when I was on day shift, less than twelve months later, I came into the station to find the night crew looking very glum.

"Morning John, had a bad night?" I said.

"Yes, you could say that. We had Andy Murphy at 0400 hrs. He had suffered a sudden cardiac arrest. There was nothing that we could do for him."

"Very sorry lads, that's a real shock," I said. "Are you both OK?"

"You know what it's like, you just have to get on with things."

Yes, I know. I've said that myself a thousand times, I thought. That is the problem for professional emergency service personnel. You are always expected to "just get on with things," but who cares for the *carers* before it is too late?

Two years after this dreadful night, I badly injured my back while lifting a very heavy patient out of an aircraft. As a result of that injury, my operational career came to an abrupt end. After months of treatment and a permanently damaged back, I returned to work but in a different capacity. This time, I went to work in our Training School. I was responsible for developing and training industrial teams in advanced first aid techniques.

First Aiders have always been an asset at times when immediate patient care was needed in the aftermath of an industrial or workplace accident. Although there was a standard national curriculum for a first aid course, I added many "tricks of the trade" to my courses which were based on years of hands-on experience.

I finally left the ambulance service in 1998 after thirty-one years of active service. I had decided to establish my own training company and carry on doing what I was told I was good at — *teaching courses.* This was purely the result of years of study linked with years of experience. The training can be taught, experience cannot — it must be gained. I enjoyed that continuation of my career immensely. It didn't take long for my business in Great Britain to become established and my client list expanded rapidly.

Then in March 2001, my wife and I became residents in Ontario, Canada and I transferred my business to Ontario. I then spent almost seventeen years delivering training all over Ontario from Ottawa to Windsor and Sudbury to Toronto. Some of those courses were specifically related to injuries that are common in what we call football in the UK and soccer for you readers in North America.

Specifically, I wrote a course which became one of the first structured training courses in football injuries and it became very popular among soccer organizations in Canada. At that time, I was delivering all levels of First Aid Courses and that took me all over Ontario. I rapidly found my way around the province both in summer and winter.

Although I never really wanted to retire, I did wrap up my training business at the end of 2017 prior to a hip replacement in January 2018. That surgery gave me a new lease on life again. Today I feel great, I feel younger than my age, and I have immensely enjoyed recording these memories to share and putting this book together for you to read.

I must say that in the writing I have found some peace and it has been therapeutic in helping me overcome my flashbacks and the symptoms of PTSD that only seemed to rear their ugly heads when I finally retired completely. My solution to life is to continue to stay active, in body and mind, and I think I will keep writing because I still have a tremendous number of stories that seem anxious to get out!

RON GILLATT

Epilogue

This book has been written with the hope that family members and friends of all emergency service professionals, and in particular those of you who know a *paramedic,* will gain some insight into what emergency work entails.

Most paramedics that I have known over the years never tell their family or friends what they have done at work. Instead, they bottle it up. It can be rewarding and great fun to be part of an emergency response team, but it can also take a tremendous toll on the members of that team, sometimes many years later. And also their families can be affected as we know.

My wife never knew what I had done when I got home at the end of a shift. I did not want to talk about it. The exposure to relentless trauma, heart-breaking scenes, and telling a loved one that their family member had in fact passed away, all of this creates a very hard veneer, frequently mistaken for callousness which, *of course,* it is not.

At the beginning of this book, I briefly mentioned that in early 2019, I was diagnosed with PTSD, a much overused term these days. It has become almost like a fashion accessory to claim to be suffering from PTSD. Even small losses or daily disappointments can sometimes be mistaken for "trauma" these days. If you know someone who has just lost or misplaced their cell phone and they are freaking out, you might even hear them say they are suffering from PTSD. I agree that many things like that can be upsetting, but I wouldn't really call that Post-Traumatic Stress Disorder!

In my own case, I woke up in the middle of the night in a cold sweat, having in my mind just completed a bad emergency call. Except I was at home in bed, not on a call, I was having a nightmare. And the memories I was seeing were from 40 and 50 years ago!

From that moment on, day and night, I found that I had a continuous *movie* playing in my head of a large number of mostly *bad jobs* that I had been involved with as a paramedic. When my wife kept insisting that something might be wrong, that I didn't seem like myself, I saw my doctor. I was diagnosed by him with PTSD, so many years after leaving the job. I was astounded that I could be affected in this way. I always thought of myself as a 'rough tough' man who could handle anything. But apparently those horrific memories had been festering, unseen and unknown inside my head, until they started to play out again in vivid colour in 2019, just after my retirement.

I decided to speak to a couple of friends who were a psychiatrist and a psychologist respectively about what was happening to me. Their advice was to write down the details of the incidents that were replaying in my head which is what I have done.

I started my career in 1967 at a time when training was virtually unheard of. Up until the late 1960s, there was a complete lack of opportunity for advancement in training. It just did not exist and it caused great frustration for me. I loved to learn and I knew there was so much more *we could have been doing* to save people in our daily work.

Finally, after a governmental study of the treatment of injured and ill patients was published in 1966, the ambulance service started to undergo a revolution in its structure and delivery of care methods. Suddenly, Ambulance Service Training Schools were established, only about six to start with in the UK but that was enough to get it going. As far as I and many of my colleagues were concerned, this was going to be the start of a transformation that would see the service brought up to date.

Training became well established very quickly and the advances were remarkable! The proof was in our daily work. We used the new equipment, techniques, protocols and training every day and it saved lives! Even CPR methods were changing with the move away from ancient resuscitation techniques to a modern procedure using manikins to practice on so everyone, even basic first-aiders, could try to perfect the skill.

As time went on, a type of *unconscious enthusiasm* for training was slowly but surely becoming established. By the early 1980s, training became even more in-depth with the opportunity for advanced paramedic training. In one of our local hospitals, the Head of Emergency Medicine was very aware as to the need for this extra training for certain crews and initiated a pilot scheme in extended training. I'm sure other groups around the world might have had to fundraise like we did in order to get the first new kinds of equipment and specialised training, but once we got started, we did not look back. A great many lives, thousands of lives, have since been saved as a result of the push for more training by crews and their respective ambulance services.

Most of the people that I worked with are either retired like me or sadly, some have passed away. I am still in touch with a small number of people that I worked with, but our numbers in the old guard are getting less and less with each passing year. Thus I wanted to document what we faced, the kind of things we pushed to achieve over those years, so the men and women in service now will understand and take pride in their jobs. Even when things are hard and when we might question if we can take another day.

One thing is for certain from my perspective. If I could do the same job again, I would jump at the chance and I think that most professional paramedics today feel this same way. Each of us have had the honour to serve our fellow citizens and make a difference. It is a *calling*, not just a *job*. Thank you for coming along on my journey through a profession that deserves respect and one that continues to grow in professionalism and capability with each passing year, saving lives every day, and saying *yes, I will help*, when no one else will go.

Acknowledgements

I would like to thank my wife, Judith, for her undying support during my years of shift work and missing so many Christmases and New Years because of my shifts. Also, and more recently, for her encouragement and unwavering support for this project.

I would also like to thank Roger, our son, for his support and all my family members for their constant help and enthusiasm throughout the writing of this book.

Also a very special thank you to my hard working and highly skilled editor, Simone Graham — without her dedication, advice and professionalism to this project, it would not have come to fruition. I am grateful also to the creative talents and advice of graphic designer Carolyn McNall who helped fashion the look for this book and who put together my website (www.rongillatt.com).

And last but not least, I would like to say thank you to all the patients that I was fortunate enough to meet throughout my career. Without you, I would not have had this most fantastic profession.